THE HOLOCAUST

The World and the Jews,
1933~1945

SEYMOUR ROSSEL

THE HOLOCAUST

The World and the Jews, 1933~1945

BEHRMAN HOUSE, INC.

ABOUT THE COVER:

The illustration on the cover is the work of Holocaust survivor Dr. Robert O. Fisch. Dr. Fisch was born in Budapest, Hungary in 1925. When he was 18 years old he was captured by the Nazis and was held in the Mauthausen and Gunzkirchen concentration camps. He was liberated by the American army in 1945, at the age of 20. With the exception of his brother, who was in Switzerland, and his mother, who hid, his entire family perished in the Holocaust. Dr. Fisch lived in Hungary until 1956, when he moved to the United States. Today he is a professor of pediatric medicine at the University of Minnesota.

Copyright © 1992 by Seymour Rossel

Designed by Richard Stalzer Associates, Ltd.

Published by Behrman House, Inc.
11 Edison Place, Springfield, NJ 07081
www.behrmanhouse.com

Library of Congress Cataloging-in-Publication Data:

Rossel, Seymour.
    The Holocaust : The World and the Jews. 1933–1945 / Seymour Rossel
       p.   cm.
    Summary: Discusses the rise of anti-Semitism in Europe, the treatment of Jews during the Holocaust, and the aftermath when the Nazi war criminals were brought to trial.
      ISBN 0–87441–526–8
      1. Holocaust, Jewish (1939–1945) — Juvenile literature.
  [1. Holocaust, Jewish (1939–1945)]
  I. Title.
D804.3.R673   1992
940.53'18—dc20

                         92-52689
                             CIP
                             AC

Manufactured in the United States of America

ACKNOWLEDGEMENTS

It was Myra Yedwab who astutely recognized the need for a documentary approach to studying the Holocaust. Behrman House and I are pleased to acknowledge her part in making this formative proposal.

The book itself grew out of a cooperative effort in which prototypes of the chapters were tested weekly for three years in the classrooms of Temple Emanu-El of Dallas, Texas. I am indebted for their help to the many teachers and young people (including my own two children—Amy and Deborah) who were a part of this process; to Karen Trager, the Director of Education; and to Sheldon Zimmerman, rabbi of the congregation. Special thanks are due to my friend and colleague, David Altshuler, who served as the editor of the book. His fine sensibilities and his unwavering support helped me past minor difficulties and kept me focused on major issues. Some years ago, that unique and meticulous historian, Lucy Dawidowicz, ז״ל, tutored me in the "reading" of photographs—studying photographs as historical evidence. Her many insights provided me with guidance with regard to the selection and use of the illustrative materials in this work. And I am grateful to Ileen McGrath for her thorough review of and fine eye for the manuscript.

— S.R.

The author and publisher gratefully acknowledge the cooperation of the following sources of photographs for this book:

A Living Memorial to the Holocaust—Museum of Jewish Heritage, 51, 52, 86, 87, 88, 89, 145; American Red Cross, 50; Anne Frank Stichting, 22, 36 (bottom), 64, 159; AP/Wide World, 60, 73, 78 (both), 79 (both), 80 (top), 83, 104, 132, 133, 172; Beit Lohamei Haghetaot, 31, 143, 147; Beth Hatefutsoth—Photo Archive, 107, 108; Bildarchiv Preussischer Kulturbesitz, 25, 84, 96, 160; Bilderdienst Suddeutscher Verlag, 72, 105; Bundesarchivs, 35; Fogelson/Florsheim Family Collection of A Living Memorial to the Holocaust—Museum of Jewish Heritage, 95; Hulton Picture Co., 80 (bottom); Imperial War Museum, London, 69; Walter Karliner, courtesy of Museum of Jewish Heritage, 98; Leo Baeck Institute, 24; Library of Congress, 77 (top); National Archives, 158, 168, 175; New York Times, 128 (top); Queensborough Public Library, 161; Georgia and Steven Solotoff, 181; Ullstein Bilderdienst, 92, 97; UPI/Bettmann Archive, 71, 77 (bottom), 103, 117, 165; Yad Vashem, 33, 43, 46, 48 (both), 49, 128 (bottom), 130, 141, 154, 171; YIVO Institute for Jewish Research, 15, 36 (top), 38, 40, 66, 90, 91, 121, 125, 127; Wiener Library, London, 65, 106; Zionist Archives, 100, 156; Zydowski Instytut Historyczny, Warsaw, 123;

"The Partisan's Hymn" ("Zog Nit Keyn Mol-Never Say") from *We are Here: Songs of the Holocaust*, compiled by Eleanor Mlotek and Malk Gottlieb, singable translations by Roslyn Bresnick-Perry (New York: The Educational Department of the Workmen's Circle and Hippocrene Books, 1983) is used by permission of The Educational Department of the Workmen's Circle.

Anne Frank: The Diary of a Young Girl by Anne Frank, © 1952 Otto H. Frank, used by permission of Doubleday, a division of Bantam Doubleday Dell Publishing Group, Inc.

Dedicated to

Hank Bloomfield

זצ"ל

A man of talent

who always encouraged

talent to develop

CONTENTS

UNIT ONE

THE HOLOCAUST

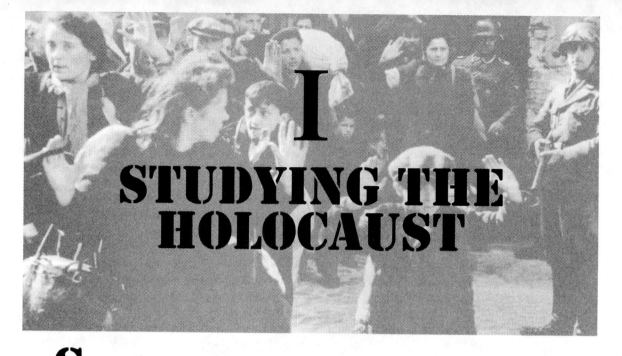

I
STUDYING THE HOLOCAUST

Six million Jews were put to death by the German state led by Adolf Hitler from 1933 to 1945, the Holocaust years. Nearly fifty years have passed since then, yet the Holocaust continues to raise important questions for Jews—and for the world at large. How could a modern state carry out the planned murder of a whole people just because they were Jews? How could the rest of the world stand by while millions of innocent people were murdered? Did Jews living in free lands do everything they could to stop the Holocaust? Did the six million Jews do everything they could to save themselves and save their world? Questions like these must be asked.

But who will explain what happened? Survivors—those who remember first-hand what happened—are few in number today, and most were children when the Holocaust took place. Listening to their experiences fills in pieces of the history. But as time passes, we turn more and more to historians to describe the Holocaust for us.

Strangely, we sometimes hear reports about professors or politicians who claim that the Holocaust never happened. A social scientist might claim that it is impossible for any group of people to have committed the murders of six million people. A politician might say that there was never a Nazi plan to kill all the Jews. A professor might claim that the story of the Holocaust was told by Jews as a part of some plot or for some evil purpose or another. The press may report the theories of these people, but such theories have no basis in fact.

The Holocaust *did* happen. There is an enormous amount of evidence to prove that it happened. And the facts of history cannot be changed. The Holocaust will continue to raise questions for many generations—and some of these questions may go unanswered forever.

This book you are reading is a book of evidence. In this book you will view actual photographs of what took place in the years of the Holocaust. In this book you will read official documents—telegrams, laws passed by governments, internal memoranda sent from one office of government to another, and signed letters written by members of government. In this book, you will also read parts of diaries, journals, and other papers left behind by eyewitnesses—people who put down on paper what they saw with their own eyes. All of these documents, writings, and photographs are first-hand evidence of what happened in the Holocaust. Every photograph, every official document, every paper tells a part of the story. Using your own eyes, the evidence in this book, and the text that ties together photographs and documents, you will discover for yourself what happened in the Holocaust.

Evidence

Take the photograph on this page, for example. This picture was taken in Warsaw, Poland in April 1943. Like many of the photographs and papers in this book, it is well-known. It has been studied time and again. As you study it now, you are doing just what each historian must do.

For a moment, imagine that you are an historian seeing this photo for the very first time. By looking at it closely, you can see that the weather outside was cold. You can see that the people with their hands in the air are Jews. How can you tell?

You probably never visited the place where this photograph was taken, so you would have to ask people who were there to tell you about the place. They would inform you that this was the central square of the Jewish ghetto in Warsaw, Poland. These Jews with their hands in the air were caught in a roundup led by Nazi soldiers like the one who stands in the dark opening at the back of the photograph. They are being guarded by German army soldiers carrying guns. The uniforms tell us which soldiers are Nazis and which are from the regular German army. Can you guess which uniforms are which?

Reading a Photograph

Take a closer look at the photograph and at the people who have been rounded up. There are children. There are women. There are old men. These might be whole families—mothers, children, grandparents—but where are the fathers? Where are the strong young men? The people in the photograph may be asking the same question. They may be asking themselves, "Will I ever see my son again?" "Will I ever see my brother again?" "Will I ever see my father again?"

The eyes of the Jews tell us more. From their faces, we can see that they are frightened. They seem to be wondering what will happen next. Will the guard suddenly raise his rifle and kill them? It is possible. It happened just that way from time to time. During a roundup, German soldiers would kill a few Jews so that the others would follow orders quickly and without question.

These are Jews. They are holding their hands in the air because they are accused of a crime. The Nazis say they are guilty of being Jewish. It is a crime punishable by death. These people are a handful of the six million Jews who died in the Holocaust. As you study this book, try to study the photographs and illustrations just as you study the written evidence. Every photograph tells a part of the story.

Photograph taken in early 1943 during the final roundup of Jews in the Warsaw ghetto. Jews caught in a roundup were loaded on railroad cattle cars and sent to concentration camps. Most of those who survived the trains and the camps were murdered in death camps.

Those Who Died

In this book, you will read many things that are difficult to believe. Stories of how Jews were treated in the concentration and death camps make us wonder how the Nazis could be so cruel. You may wonder how so many innocent people could be put to death. You are not alone. Even those who survived the Holocaust found it difficult to believe that these events were real.

Yet, the nearly six million Jews who died in the Holocaust years (1939-1945) were very real. They had families; they worked or attended school; they took walks in parks, they went to the movies on Saturday nights, visited museums, and played football; they listened to music, danced and sang, studied and taught, ate in restaurants, shopped in department stores, and gave parties in their homes. Each of them had hopes, feelings, wishes, and needs; each of them had parents, friends, and relatives.

JEWS WHO DIED IN THE HOLOCAUST	
Polish and Russian Jews	4,565,000
German Jews	125,000
Austrian Jews	65,000
Czechoslovakian Jews	277,000
Hungarian Jews	402,000
French Jews	83,000
Belgian Jews	24,000
Jews of Luxembourg	700
Italian Jews	7,500
Jews of the Netherlands	106,000
Norwegian Jews	760
Rumanian Jews	40,000
Yugoslavian Jews	60,000
Greek Jews	65,000
TOTAL LOSS	**5,820,960**

As many as six million Jews died between 1939 and 1945, the years of the Holocaust.

Source: *Encyclopedia Judaica*, Vol 8, p. 889

Suddenly their tomorrows were taken from them. We can never know what their futures might have meant to us—to all humanity. We are missing the books, the plays, the movies, the songs, and the poetry they might have written. We are missing the statues they might have sculpted and the paintings they might have painted. We are missing their scientific research. We are missing their teachings and their ideas. We are missing the inventions they might have invented, the speeches they might have given, even the questions they might have asked.

And we are missing the children they might have brought into the world. Any one of the Jews who died in the Holocaust might have been your great-aunt or great-uncle. Any one of their children might have been your grandmother or grandfather. If not for the Holocaust, you might have had cousins upon cousins in Europe.

Jewish tradition (*Avot de Rabbi Natan 31*) teaches that when a life is taken, it is as if an entire world is lost. Why? Because along with losing a person we lose all the life that would come from that person, from that time to the end of time.

Reasons for Studying the Holocaust

The Holocaust changed history—Jewish history and world history. Today, more than a generation later, we still do not have a complete understanding of this single event. That is one reason for continuing to study the evidence itself, for continually reviewing the facts and retelling the history of the Holocaust.

Knowing what the Jewish world of Europe was like before the Holocaust is a second reason for our study. Since this world was destroyed, we have to study it as history if we are to know anything about it.

The story of the destruction is a tragic one. It does not have a simple, happy ending. Still, it is a bit like looking up into the sky on a dark night. Here and there, a star shines through. Here and there, the tragedy is less because the human heart spoke freely and truly. Here and there, many stories speak of bravery and courage. Here and there, many stories tell of people who cared deeply for others and reached out to help. To seek these lights in the darkness is another reason to study the Holocaust. Moments of bravery and courage teach us how Jews and other good human beings should behave and act in troubled times.

Last but not least, we must also confront the tragedy of the Holocaust. We must gaze deeply into the darkness to learn the truth about evil. If we are to become better human beings—and better Jews—we need to know about what is bad and how to prevent it. We need to learn the lessons that the Holocaust has to teach us. We need to remember these lessons and repeat them from one generation to another. Even though they are hard memories and brutal ones, they are a part of our history as Jews, a part of us.

To learn these lessons—to know what happened, and how it happened—we must look back to that moment when the National Socialist German Workers' Party (known by its initials as the Nazi Party) turned the full force of the German government against the Jewish people.

REVIEW | ISSUES

■ The plan of this book is simple. The first unit—**The Holocaust**—tells what happened to the Jews of Europe from 1933 to 1945. The second unit—**The World and the Jews**—asks some of the pressing questions: Why were the Jews selected to be Hitler's victims? Who were the Nazis and what kind of leaders did they follow? How did the Nazis come to control the government of Germany and how did they organize the slaughter of the Jews? What was the Jewish world in Europe like before the Holocaust? How did Jews outside of Europe learn about the Holocaust and what did they do once they knew? The third unit—**Resistance, Rescue, and Justice**—tells of the bravery and courage of the victims and those who risked their lives to rescue them. It also speaks of the aftermath of the Holocaust. What happened to the remaining Jews in Europe—the Holocaust survivors—when the war ended? What happened to the Nazis after the war? How has the Holocaust changed Jewish history? And how has the Holocaust changed the history of the world?

■ Each chapter presents evidence to show what happened and how. Each chapter ends with a brief review and a few issues for you to consider. From this point forward, the study of the issues and the evidence is up to you. You are the historian.

■ The photograph printed in this chapter was introduced in evidence at the War Crimes trials held in Nuremberg in 1945 (see Chapter 14.)

1. Why do you think this photograph was selected as evidence? What is different about it from other photographs?

2. What conclusions can you draw from the photograph? What other things do you want to know after looking at it?

■ Look through the whole book, studying a few of the photographs in the way that the chapter describes.

3. See how much you can learn by just "reading" a photograph completely, the way historians do.

■ The chapter says that if the Holocaust had not occurred, you might have countless relatives in Europe today.

4. Ask your parents about this. Did you have relatives who perished in the Holocaust? Do they remember any stories about the Holocaust that they were told?

■ Review the reasons given for the study of the Holocaust.

5. Do you agree with all these reasons? Are there any others which have not been mentioned?

6. Which do you think is the most important?

II
THE HOLOCAUST BEGINS

In 1938, Germany's government was led by Adolf Hitler and the Nazi Party. Hitler and the Nazis had been in power in Germany for five years. In that time they passed many anti-Jewish laws. They had done much to encourage anti-Semitism—hatred of the Jews. Jewish life in Germany had become more and more difficult, more and more unbearable. It seemed that the Nazis wanted to force every Jew to leave Germany. But, for many reasons, most German Jews believed that the Hitler years would pass. Despite the anti-Semitism and anti-Jewish laws, most German Jews remained loyal to Germany and chose to stay.

Since most German Jews refused to leave, Hitler turned his attention to Jews inside Germany who were not German citizens. Most of these people were Jews from eastern Europe. They lived scattered throughout Germany in cities like Leipzig, Cologne, Dusseldorf, Essen, and Bremen. In October, 1938, eighteen thousand eastern European Jews were rounded up in Germany by Nazi storm troopers and sent by truck and train to the German-Polish border.

One of the Jews caught in the roundup was Zindel Grynszpan. Zindel was born in Poland in 1886. In 1911, he moved his family to Hanover, Germany. He, his wife, his daughter, and one son were all transported from Hanover to the border. His oldest son, Hirsch, had moved to Paris in 1936. Zindel remembered:

> When we reached the border, we were searched to see if anybody had any money, and anybody who had more than ten marks, the balance was taken from him. This was the German law. No more than ten marks could be taken out of Germany. . . .
>
> Zindel Grynszpan in Gilbert, *The Holocaust*, p. 67.

On October 27, 1938, the Nazi storm troopers marched the eastern European Jews two kilometers (about one mile) to the Polish border. Then they forced the Jews to cross the border.

> The SS men were whipping us, those who lingered they hit, and blood was flowing on the road. . . . They treated us in a most barbaric fashion—this was the first time that I'd ever seen the wild barbarism of the Germans.
>
> They shouted at us, "Run! Run!" I myself received a blow and I fell in the ditch. My son helped me, and he said, "Run, run, dad—otherwise you'll die!". . . The rain was driving hard, people were fainting—some suffered heart attacks; on all sides one saw old men and women. Our suffering was great—there was no food. . . .
>
> Zindel Grynszpan in Gilbert, *The Holocaust*, p. 68.

Zindel and his family had been thrown out of Germany. Zindel was depressed and upset. He wrote a postcard to one of his sons, Hirsch Grynszpan, who was living in Paris, telling him what had happened.

When Hirsch received his father's postcard, he was furious. On November 6, 1938, Hirsch Grynszpan went to the German Embassy in Paris and demanded to see the ambassador. A German official named Ernst von Rath walked toward Hirsch. In a fit of anger, Hirsch drew a pistol from his pocket and shot von Rath, who died three days later.

The Nazis claimed that the assassination of von Rath was part of a world Jewish plot against Germany. In the three days following the shooting, the Nazis planned their revenge.

Action Against the Jews

Berlin, Germany: Thursday, November 9, 1938. Everything seemed peaceful in the Jewish neighborhood. Mothers walked children to school and shopkeepers opened stores for business. Lawyers and doctors greeted secretaries and nurses and went in to speak with clients and patients.

The Jews of Berlin were not altogether happy. Some were out of work, looking for new jobs. A recent law forbade government offices from employing Jews. Those Jews who had worked in government offices were now seeking work elsewhere. Another law made it a crime for young non-Jews to work as maids in Jewish households. On this Thursday in 1938, many Jews were trying to find young Jewish girls who might be willing to do housework and take care of small children.

Another law removed citizenship rights from German Jews. But on this November day that seemed to make very little difference. There were no elections coming up. And most Jews did not feel threatened. They were loyal German citizens; and they were sure that one day soon Adolf Hitler and his Nazi Party would be voted out of office and everything would return to normal.

Saturday in the Jewish Quarter in Berlin. Jews attend synagogue in the peaceful days before the Nazi rise to power.

Yet even as they worked at their everyday jobs and went about their everyday business, the telegraph wires were carrying a message that would change their lives. Here is the message sent from Gestapo headquarters:

Berlin No. 234 404 9.11.2355

To all Gestapo Stations and Gestapo District Stations

To Officer or Deputy

This teleprinter message is to be delivered without delay

1. At very short notice *Aktionen* against the Jews, especially against their synagogues, will take place throughout the whole of Germany. They are not to be hindered. In conjunction with the

police, however, it is to be ensured that looting and other such excesses can be prevented.

2. If important archive material is in synagogues, this is to be taken into safekeeping by an immediate measure.

3. Preparations are to be made for the arrest of between 20,000 and 30,000 Jews in the Reich [the German state]. Wealthy Jews in particular are to be selected. More detailed instructions will be issued in the course of this night.

4. Should, in the forthcoming *Aktionen*, Jews be found in possession of weapons, the most severe measures are to be taken. SS Reserves as well as the General SS can be mobilized in the total *Aktionen*. The direction of the *Aktionen* by the Gestapo is in any case to be ensured by appropriate measures.

Gestapo II Mueller

This teleprinter message is secret.

Cited in Schoenberner, *The Yellow Star*, p. 12.

Heinrich Mueller ("Gestapo II Mueller") was the head of the political police, the Gestapo. He was ordered to send the telegram by Reinhard Heydrich and Heinrich Himmler, two top officials of the Nazi Party. It was clear that this was an order from the top, an order that had the blessing, if not the signature, of Hitler himself. So the political police got ready for their first anti-Jewish *Aktionen*—planned "actions" against the synagogues of Germany.

Official records tell us what happened next. The rioting began that evening. It continued for the next two days. Synagogues were burned. The windows of Jewish stores were broken. Many Germans stood by and watched. Some Germans broke into Jewish stores, taking whatever they could grab, whatever they could stuff into their pockets or carry off. The regular police watched. When a Jew tried to stop the looting of a store or put out a synagogue fire, the police arrested him. Fire brigades kept the fires from spreading to non-Jewish homes. But they did nothing to stop synagogues and Jewish homes from burning. On November 10, Heydrich sent another telegram to the Gestapo stations saying:

As soon as the night's events make police inspectors available, there will be an opportunity to arrest as many Jews—preferably those who are rich—as the jails can hold. Male Jews who are in good health, and not too old, are to be arrested first. After the arrests, immediate contact is to be made with the nearest concentration camps for the speedy jailing of the Jews.

Cited in Poliakov, *Harvest of Hate*, p. 17.

In cities throughout Germany the Gestapo broke into Jewish homes, arresting husbands and fathers. "Why?" the Jews cried. "What is my crime?" The answer was: Jews are accused of starting the riots.

Kristallnacht. **Flames rise from a synagogue in Baden-Baden. Some Jews died bravely trying to rescue Torah scrolls and other sacred books.**

November 11. Heydrich sent his first report to Hermann Goering, one of Hitler's chief advisors:

> At this time, the extent to which Jewish stores and apartments were sacked cannot yet be established. The figures already known are: 815 stores demolished, 29 warehouses burned, 171 houses set on fire; this represents only a part of the havoc. The

great majority of the reports that have reached us are limited to such generalizations as "destruction of numerous stores" or "destruction of the majority of stores." One hundred ninety-one synagogues have been set on fire and 76 completely destroyed; 20,000 Jews have been arrested, along with 7 Aryans [Germans] and 3 foreigners; 36 Jews have been assassinated, 36 seriously wounded.

Nuremberg Trial Document PS 3058.

So many shop windows were broken that it would take two years for the plate glass factories in Belgium to replace them all.

The Air Ministry Conference

November 12. Goering called a conference at the Air Ministry Building to discuss the *Aktionen* against the Jews. Many top Nazi officials were there. Goering started the session by saying:

> Gentlemen, today's meeting is of decisive importance. I have received a letter. . . by order of the Fuhrer [Adolf Hitler], asking that the Jewish question be treated in its entirety and settled in some way. Yesterday the Fuhrer telephoned me to point out again that decisive measures must be undertaken in a coordinated manner.

Nuremberg Trial Document PS 1816

The Nazis discussed the best ways to separate the Jews of Germany from their businesses, their factories, and their real estate. Then a larger question was raised. So much had been destroyed in the last two days that the Jews would be filing many claims against German and international insurance companies. How could they keep the Jews from getting money back to pay for these damages? They sent for an insurance expert to come and talk with them. While they waited for the insurance expert to arrive, the Nazi Minister of Propaganda Joseph Goebbels spoke to the group.

Goebbels: In almost every German city synagogues have been burned. The land on which they stood can be used in many different ways; some cities want to convert the land into parks; others want to build on it.

Goering: How many synagogues were actually set afire?

Heydrich: One hundred and one synagogues were burned, 76 demolished; 7,500 stores were destroyed.

Goebbels: I believe this gives us an opportunity to dissolve the synagogues. All those not completely intact must be torn down by the Jews themselves. . . . Moreover, I think it necessary to issue an ordinance forbidding Jews to attend German theaters, movies, and circuses. . . . It is not possible to allow Jews to sit beside Germans. . . . Furthermore, they must be removed from public view. . . for example [on trains].

Goering: . . . There will be only one Jewish car. If it is full, the other Jews must stay at home.

Goebbels: And suppose. . . there are two Jews on the train, and the other cars are crowded. These two Jews, then, have a car to themselves. We should therefore announce that Jews cannot sit until all Germans are seated.

Goering: I wouldn't go to the trouble to announce it, but I'd give the Jews a car or a section to themselves. If the train is really full, as you say, believe me, I don't need a law. The Jew will be thrown out, even if he has to sit by himself in the toilet for the whole trip.

Goebbels: . . . Another ordinance should forbid Jews to visit German spas, beaches, and summer resorts. . . . I wonder if it isn't necessary to keep Jews out of German parks.

Goering: Well, we'll set aside a certain part of the park for the Jews. [Park Rangers] will take care of putting animals there that look like Jews. . . .

Goebbels: Finally, we must consider the following: There are actually still cases of Jewish children attending German schools. I think this is impossible. It is out of the question for my boy to sit beside a Jew in a German high school while he is being taught German history. It is absolutely necessary to bar Jews from German schools. Let them take care of raising their own community.

Nuremberg Trial Document PS 1816

Paying for the Damage

After a while, the insurance expert arrived. He said that precious German money would have to be spent to settle the claims of the Jewish businesses that had been destroyed. Most of the money would have to be paid to repair the broken window glass. Plate glass for shop windows came only from Belgium. It might take two years for the Belgian factories to manufacture enough plate glass just to replace the many shop windows that had been broken! And all that German money would have to be spent in Belgium! The official record shows that Goering was very disturbed by this. Goering said, "I would rather you had slaughtered 200 Jews than destroyed such valuable property."

It did not take long for the Nazis to find a solution to their problem. The Jews themselves would pay the cost of the damages! At last, the *Aktion* had a name. It was named for the broken shop windows—*Kristallnacht*—"The Night of Broken Glass." The discussion continued:

> **Heydrich:** I should like to make some suggestions about isolating [the Jews]. . . . Every Jew will have to wear a special badge!. . . I propose furthermore that the Jews be deprived of all personal privileges, such as driver's licenses, and forbidden to own automobiles, for a Jew does not have the right to be a danger to Aryan [German] lives. . . and so in the case of hospitals. A Jew can't stay in the same hospital with Aryans.
>
> **Goering:** Aren't there any Jewish hospitals. . . ? (*Cries:* Yes, there are!) All these things must be investigated thoroughly. They must be done away with one after another. . . . One more question, gentlemen. What would you say if I proclaimed today that a fine of one billion would be imposed on the Jews as a contribution?. . . That is going to hit home. I must say it again: I shouldn't care to be a Jew in Germany!
>
> **Von Krosigk:** We must do everything to send the Jews away. . . . I can imagine that the prospect of being driven into ghettos will not be a very pleasant one. The goal must then be, as Heydrich said: "Clear out [as many Jews] as we can!"
>
> **Goering:** If [we] should later. . . become involved in a war, it goes without saying that we in Germany shall have to consider settling our accounts in a big way with the Jews. . . . Furthermore, the Fuhrer [Hitler]. . . explained it to me on November 9. That's the only way to do it. He wants to say to the other countries: "Why are you always talking about the Jews? Take them!"
>
> Nuremberg Trial Document PS 1816.

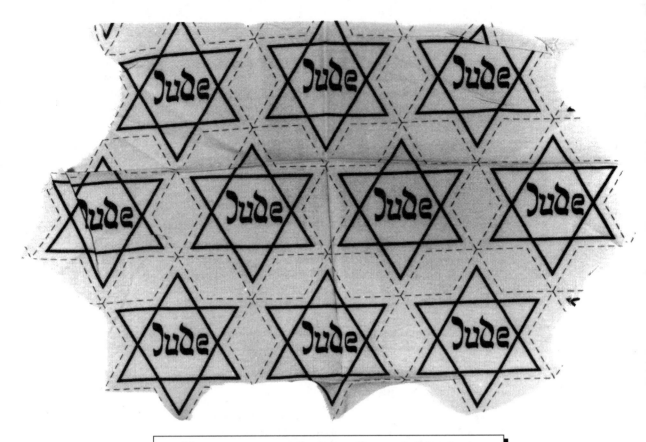

Jewish stars were stamped out on yellow material and cut. Jews were forced to buy stars like these and sew them on all their clothing.

REVIEW | ISSUES

■ *Kristallnacht* was the first major "action" in the Holocaust. From the meeting at the Air Ministry Conference, you have already heard how Nazis felt about the Jews of Germany. Before the Night of Broken Glass, Hitler had already come to power. The German government had already passed anti-Jewish laws.

■ After the Night of Broken Glass, events moved quickly. Within a few short years, six million Jews were murdered. *Kristallnacht* was a hint of what was soon to come.

■ Review the photographs in the chapter.
1. What can you learn from these photos? Why was each of them included?

■ In the *Kristallnacht Aktionen*, both people and property were destroyed. Use the evidence presented in the chapter to answer:
2. Which of these was more important to the Jews? Which was more important to the Nazis?
3. What does this tell you about the Nazis' view of the value of life?

■ Review the remarks made by Nazi Minister of Propaganda Joseph Goebbels and by Hermann Goering.
4. What kind of a person was Goebbels? What kind of person was Goering? What position did Goering hold in the government?

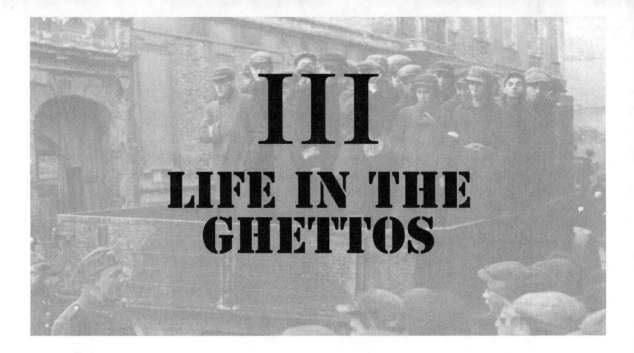

III
LIFE IN THE GHETTOS

World War II began on September 1, 1939. Within three weeks, the German army conquered Poland. The Nazis suddenly controlled 1,700,000 Polish Jews, more than half the total Jewish population of Poland. The other 1,600,000 Jews lived in eastern Poland, which was now claimed by Russia. Before the war, the Nazis tried to force Jews to leave German soil and occupied lands. Now that war was officially declared, the Germans called the Jews "enemies of the Aryan race and the Third Reich [Hitler's German state]."

By September 1939, Reinhard Heydrich had already planned and ordered the next step that Jews would be forced to take.

> **SECRET** *Berlin: September 21, 1939*
> *To:* Chiefs of all Einsatzgruppen of the Security Police
> *Subject:* Jewish question in the occupied territory
>
> I refer to the conference held in Berlin today. . . .
>
> For the time being, the first [step toward] the final aim is the concentration of the Jews from the countryside into the larger cities. This is to be carried out with all speed. . . .
>
> In each Jewish community, a Council of Jewish Elders is to be set up. . . . The Councils of Elders are to be informed of the dates and deadlines. . . . They are then to be made personally responsible for the departure of the Jews from the countryside. . . . For general reasons of security, the concentration of Jews in the cities will probably necessitate orders altogether barring Jews from certain sections of the cities, or, for example, forbidding them to leave the ghetto. . . .
>
> Heydrich
>
> Cited in Dawidowicz, *A Holocaust Reader*, pp. 59-64.

From small towns and villages, Jews were sent by rail to the larger cities. At first, barbed wire was stretched across the city streets to make a "Jewish section" or ghetto. Later, brick walls were built to cage the Jews inside the ghetto. In the end, a single ghetto like the one in Warsaw might contain hundreds of thousands of Jews within a few city blocks. One Nazi report claimed that as many as seven Jews lived in each room of the buildings inside the Warsaw ghetto.

Starvation

The greatest danger during the early years of the ghettos was starvation. Men fought one another for a raw potato. Mothers traded all their possessions for food for their children, and even so babies died for lack of food. In the end, each Jew had to live a whole month on only 2 pounds of bread, 9 ounces of sugar, 3½ ounces of jam, and 1¾ ounces of fat. Meat and cheese were almost impossible to find.

The Jews of Warsaw were enclosed in a ghetto. The wall was made two bricks deep, and sharp pieces of glass were placed between the bricks to keep anyone from climbing out.

GHETTOS AND CONCENTRATION CAMPS

Boundary of Poland until
September 1939

German-Russian border,
1939–June 1941

✗ Death camps (names underlined)

• Ghettos

Baltic Sea

LATVIA

Riga

LITHUANIA

Kovno

Vilna

Minsk

Danzig
(Gdansk)

EAST
PRUSSIA

Grodno

SOVIET

GERMANY

Bialystok

Baranowicze

UNION

Poznan

✗ Chelmno

✗ Treblinka

Brest

Pinsk

Lodz

WARSAW

Radom

Sobibor ✗

Breslau

✗ Lublin
Majdanek

Dubno

Czestochowa

Belzec ✗

Oswiecim

Cracow

UKRAINE

Auschwitz-
Birkenau ✗

Przemysl

Lvov

Ternopol

CZECHOSLOVAKIA

HUNGARY

ROMANIA

Germany and Russia split Poland into two major parts. In western Poland, the Nazis set up ghettos in major cities like Lodz and Warsaw. Later, death camps like Auschwitz and Treblinka were built.

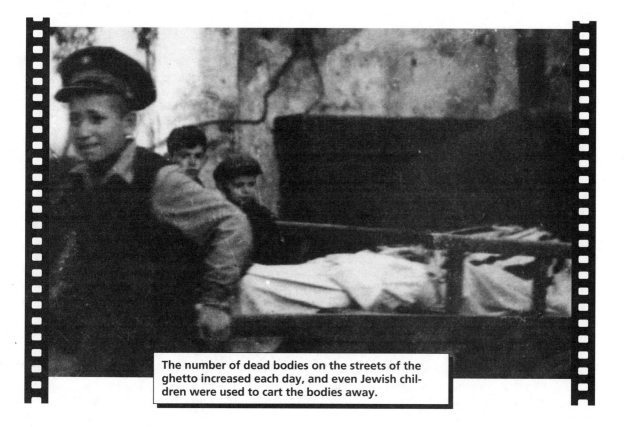

The number of dead bodies on the streets of the ghetto increased each day, and even Jewish children were used to cart the bodies away.

Imprisoned in the Warsaw ghetto, Professor Ludwik Hirszfeld wrote in his diary:

> The streets are so over-populated, it is difficult to push one's way through. . . . There are always countless children inside the ghetto. . . . Not all the German guards are murderers and executioners, but unfortunately, many of them do not hesitate to take up their guns and fire at the children. Every day—it is almost unbeliev-able—children are taken to hospital with gunshot wounds.
>
> All Jews must wear the armband with its Star of David. The chil-dren are the only exceptions, and this makes it easier for them to smuggle food in. . . . Horrifying sights are to be seen every day. . . . One sees people dying, lying with arms and legs outstretched, in the middle of the road. Their legs are bloated, often frost-bitten, and their faces distorted with pain. . . .
>
> I once asked a little girl: "What would you like to be?" "A dog," she answered, "because the guards like dogs."
>
> Ludwik Hirszfeld in Schoenberner, *The Yellow Star*, p. 51.

During the month of January 1941, nearly two thousand Jews died of starvation in the Warsaw ghetto. The Polish historian Emanuel Ringel-blum kept a diary noting what he saw and heard. He interviewed many Jews, writing down what they told him, hoping to one day help historians tell the story of the Warsaw ghetto. His diaries survived the war and tell us much about everyday life inside the ghetto. On February 28, 1941 he wrote:

> Almost daily people are falling dead or unconscious in the middle of the street. It no longer makes so direct an impression. [The streets are] forever full of newly arrived refugees. . . . Terrible case of a three-year-old refugee child. [On the way to Warsaw] the guard threw the child into the snow. Its mother jumped off the wagon and tried to save the child. The guard threatened her with a revolver. The mother insisted life was worthless for her without her child. Then the guard threatened to shoot all the Jews in the wagon. The mother arrived in Warsaw, and here went out of her mind.
>
> Emanuel Ringelblum,
> *Notes from the Warsaw Ghetto*, pp. 130-132.

As the German armies conquered more territory, more Jews were sent to the ghettos. Food became an ever greater problem. Death from starvation was commonplace. Jews in the ghetto were so weak that their bodies could not fight off diseases and a plague of spotted fever took hold, causing many additional deaths.

A German report issued in 1941 estimated that it would take only five more years to complete the total starvation of the whole Jewish ghetto in Warsaw. The Nazis were already planning ways to speed up the process.

Forced Labor

As Jews entered the ghettos, the Nazis took away their valuable possessions. Despite this, they made regular raids inside the ghettos looking for fur coats, gold watches, and diamond rings they might have missed. Nazis would whip, cut off beards, even murder some Jews caught in their raids. One Jewish woman recalled how the Nazis stormed into a meeting of her house committee one night, forced the Jews to strip naked, then threatened them all at gunpoint, telling them to "cough up" their diamonds and dollars. The horrible threats continued from about 11 p.m. to 2 a.m., when the Nazis left, carrying only a few watches and some loose change. There were no diamonds or dollars among the committee members.

Because their own men were in the military, the Germans often needed extra workers for clothing and ammunition factories. From time to time, German soldiers would raid the ghetto to grab the stronger young men for a day's work. The Jewish Council in Warsaw wanted to end the terror caused by these raids. So they offered to help the Germans by setting up regular places for labor teams to gather and choosing men to form the labor gangs. The Germans were pleased to accept this plan, since it made their roundup of laborers much more efficient. The Jews were pleased to work, since workers were often paid small amounts or even fed by the Nazis.

Later, labor camps were set up for larger projects. Food in the labor camps was no more than watery soup, some bread, potatoes, and margarine. Jews looked forward to days when small portions of leftover meat were declared unfit to eat by the German army and sent to the prisoners.

When labor was no longer needed at one camp, the prisoners were placed on trains and sent to another camp. The laborers might never see their homes again. One time a train of 900 left a labor camp, only to arrive at the next labor camp with only 500 Jews aboard. The head of the second camp wrote:

> Since they could not very well have been shot in such large numbers, I have heard suspicions that perhaps these Jews had been released against payment of some kind of money.
>
> Cited in Hilberg, *The Destruction of the European Jews*, p. 166.

This official went on to say that the second train of 900 laborers arrived with no one missing. He added that most of the Jews on the second train were from faraway Lublin. It would be nearly impossible, he added, to get them back to Lublin.

Forced labor gangs were gathered by the Nazis to do work outside the ghettos. Many men volunteered for the small pay or the extra food rations that the Nazis often gave to the workers.

The Judenraete

The Jewish Councils, or *Judenraete*, were formed by the Nazis at the beginning of the ghetto period. They were charged with two duties—to carry out Nazi orders, and to take care of the poor and needy within the ghettos. Popular Jewish leaders were carefully chosen for positions on the *Judenraete*. When they refused to carry out Nazi orders, they were often taken out and shot.

The Jewish community provided for children through the Children's Kitchen and a home for orphans.

A singing lesson at the Boys' Boarding School in Warsaw.

In some places, the Jews came to hate their *Judenraete* and their leaders. In the Lodz ghetto, for example, one leader by the name of Rumkowski was sometimes sarcastically called "the King of the Jews." And in other ghettos, too, the members of the *Judenraete* were often very comfortable when compared with the average Jew. The average ghetto Jew in these places felt that the *Judenraete* were betraying the Jewish people, collaborating with the Nazis for their own gain.

For the most part, however, the *Judenraete* took the business of Jewish welfare seriously. They established special committees to look after the many needs of the Jewish community. One report issued in Vilna in 1942 listed some areas of need:

PROGRAM OF INNOVATIONS PLANNED FOR OCTOBER

(1) Public Health. . .
(2) Hospital. . .
(3) Clinic. . .
(4) Children's Consultation [Agency]. . .
(5) Children's Home. . .
(6) Day Care Center. . .
(7) Vitamin Laboratory. . .

Cited in Dawidowicz, *A Holocaust Reader*, pp. 185-186.

Almost always, the *Judenraete* attempted to help the many children. Estimates said that one-fourth of the total Jewish population was made up of children, and eyewitnesses constantly remarked that children were to be seen everywhere in the ghettos. Of the many children's homes and child welfare projects, the most famous was run by the Warsaw Jewish teacher, Janusz Korczak. In February 1940 Korczak wrote, "I assert with great joy that with a few exceptions man is a creature of understanding and goodness. Not just 100, but 150 [children] are in the Dom Sierot [orphanage]." Yet he constantly needed more money for his growing orphanage. In March 1940, in an appeal for more funds, he told about the work of the orphanage:

> The latest child who was admitted here after quarantine in the hospital: his father disappeared without a trace; his mother and his sister were killed by a bomb before his eyes. The injury to his foot has not yet healed. With the one eye that remains to him after the explosion he will view the world. We coax a smile upon his tormented face. Peaceably they run about and play, the children who came recently with wounds on their frozen fingers and toes, abused, hungry, hunted.

Janusz Korczak in Dawidowicz, *A Holocaust Reader*, p. 194.

On August 5, 1942, Korczak was ordered to take the children to a waiting train. He dressed the children in their "best" *shabbat* clothing and led them singing through the streets of Warsaw. The children were not afraid because their beloved "doctor" was going with them. Korczak, aged 64, and all the children of his Dom Sierot orphanage, were sent to Treblinka. There they were put to death in the gas chambers.

Daily Life in the Ghettos

Religious life was strong in the ghettos. Traditional Jews tried to continue observing the *mitzvot*, as they had done in their small towns and villages. Of course, the Nazis had outlawed synagogues and religion, so the Jews gathered and prayed secretly. Boys continued studying for bar mitzvah, and young men continued studying to become rabbis and scholars. On August 12, 1940, Chaim Kaplan, another historian of the Warsaw ghetto, wrote that "public prayer in these dangerous times is a forbidden act. Anyone caught in this crime is doomed to severe punishment. If you will, it is even sabotage and anyone engaging in sabotage is subject to execution."

A street singer plays his mandolin as other children gather around him. Even in the worst days of the ghetto, people continued to study music and art, continued to write, and continued to try to enjoy life.

But Jews met that evening to observe *Tisha B'Av*, the fast day devoted to remembering the destruction of the Temple. There were 600 secret congregations in Warsaw alone. They met in cellars, in attics, in back rooms. Men stood guard watching for Nazi troops. Special prayers were even added to the daily service. For Passover, beet juice sweetened with saccharine was used instead of wine. The rabbis of the Holocaust agreed that many observances could be set aside because of the difficulties of the ghetto.

While many Jews continued to observe religious rituals and festivals, others had not been religious even before the Holocaust, and some lost their faith entirely during the Holocaust years. These Jews relied more on other activities available to all the people of the ghetto, religious or not.

Teaching was done in secret. In times of danger, children hid their books inside their jackets. Each building became a miniature center for the arts. Actors, musicians, singers, comics, and dancers performed for small groups everywhere in the ghettos. The most popular adult study was English language courses. Larger communities like Vilna organized donated books into lending libraries. Books were smuggled from one building to another so that people could continue reading and enjoying them.

Children were everywhere—always in need of food, always in need of clothing. Many had lost their parents. Others were the breadwinners for their whole families, slipping through sewers and cracks in the wall, smuggling small bits of food into the ghetto.

REVIEW | ISSUES

■ The Jews of Europe were trapped by the speed with which the German armies overran Poland and most of Europe. The Nazis created ghettos—gathering the Jews into small areas in the larger cities. By cutting off most food supplies to the ghetto, the Nazis set out to starve the Jews to death. But they were not pleased by the length of time starvation took. They began seeking out faster ways to destroy Jewish lives, even as they used Jewish labor to help them in their war efforts. Meanwhile, Jews continued to find ways of making life bearable, even enjoyable.

■ Resisting the Nazis was not an easy thing to do. The Nazis were specialists in terror and organization. Yet the Jews of the ghettos resisted in many ways.

1. Consider the story of Janusz Korczak. In what ways did Korczak resist the Nazis? Korczak and all the children of his orphanage died at Treblinka. Was his resistance successful?

2. In the Talmud (*Shevuot* 39a) it is written that "All Jews are responsible for one another." In what way did the Jews of the ghetto act out this basic Jewish value?

3. Why do you think that the Jews of the ghettos continued preparing for the future even as the Nazis were destroying them?

■ Review the material about the *Judenraete*, the Jewish Councils.

4. What is your impression of the *Judenraete*? Were they generally good leaders? What mistakes do you think they made?

5. How would you feel if you were a member of one of the *Judenraete*? How would you feel about the *Judenraete* if you were a survivor of the ghettos?

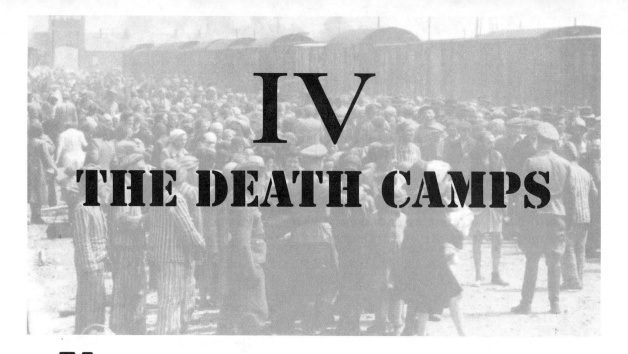

IV

THE DEATH CAMPS

No one is quite certain of the exact moment when the Nazis decided to murder the Jews. Yet it was agreed by all Nazi officials that the solution of the Jewish Question was a primary goal of the German war effort. As early as January 1939, Hitler confided his plan to the Czech foreign minister: "We are going to destroy the Jews." And in his speech to the *Reichstag*—the German congress—at the end of the month, he gave the news to the nation officially.

> I have often been a prophet in my life and was generally laughed at. During my struggle for power, the Jews primarily received with laughter my prophecies that I would someday assume the leadership of the state. . . and then, among many other things, achieve a solution of the Jewish problem. I suppose [that the laughter] of Jewry in Germany is now choking in their throats.
>
> Today I will be a prophet again: If international finance Jewry. . . should succeed once more in plunging the peoples into a world war, then the consequence will be. . . the destruction of the Jewish race in Europe.
>
> Adolf Hitler in Dawidowicz, *The War Against the Jews*, p. 142.

This was Hitler's declaration of war against the Jews. Following Hitler's lead, Himmler, Heydrich, and other top Nazi officials publicly referred to the Jews as "enemies of the state." The Nazis believed that the Jews were "subhuman"; in speeches they compared the Jews to a disease.

In October 1939 Heydrich appointed SS major Adolf Eichmann to take over the Berlin desk for Jewish Affairs and Evacuation Affairs. Eichmann was already well-known for forcing 145,000 Jews to flee Austria. He was called an "expert" in Jewish matters. He had visited Palestine, studied the Jewish religion, and even taken lessons in the Hebrew language.

His new job gave Eichmann nearly absolute power over the fate of the Jews. From behind his desk in a small office in Berlin, he made decisions that resulted in the death of six million Jews.

Before the war began, the Nazis had used the word "evacuation" to mean "expulsion." They tried many ways of repeating Eichmann's Austrian success throughout the German-ruled lands. From 1941 onward, they used the word "evacuation" to mean sending Jews to the death camps.

Adolf Hitler, dictator of Germany from 1933 to 1945.

Einsatzgruppen

There may have been a master plan to destroy all Jews, but from 1939-41, the Nazis concentrated mainly on moving the Jews to the larger cities in the East and allowing them to starve to death in the ghettos. In 1941, however, as plans were being finalized for the invasion of Russia, three thousand men were picked and formed into four special groups called *Einsatzgruppen* ("Special Duty Groups"). As part of their training, Heydrich taught them that:

> Judaism in the East is the source of Bolshevism and must therefore be wiped out in accordance with the Fuehrer's aims.
>
> Reinhard Heydrich in Dawidowicz,
> *The War Against the Jews*, p. 167.

When the German armies attacked Russia in June 1941, the *Einsatzgruppen* followed close behind. As was later explained by one of its leaders, each unit

> would enter a village or city and order the prominent Jewish citizens to call together all Jews for the purpose of resettlement. They were requested to hand over their valuables to the leader of the unit, and shortly before the execution to surrender their outer clothing. The men, women, and children were led to a place of execution which in most cases was located next to a more deeply excavated anti-tank ditch. Then they were shot, kneeling or standing, and corpses thrown into the ditch.
>
> SS Colonel Jaeger in Dawidowicz,
> *The War Against the Jews*, p. 170.

In all, nearly 800,000 eastern European Jews were murdered by the *Einsatzgruppen*. Some 35,000 Jews were murdered in the Babi Yar ravine near Kiev. This was the single largest massacre of the war. Reports of the actions were regularly sent back to Berlin. One commander noted that Lithuanians were so ready to help the *Einsatzgruppen* that Kovno, Lithuania "was . . . a shooter's paradise." Several unit leaders were worried, however. They said that some Nazi machine-gunners were uncomfortable with killing so many people—a few had even had sleepless nights. Heydrich and Eichmann continued to feel that the destruction was going too slowly. They were already searching for a quicker way.

The Euthanasia Program

The quicker way was already being used by another department of the Nazi government. As a soldier in World War I, Adolf Hitler had been caught in a gas attack. He remembered the bitter, choking feeling of the gas and the fear that gripped him. In 1939, he started a euthanasia ("mercy killing") program—putting to death German children who were mentally ill or physically handicapped. At first, doctors killed these "imperfect Aryans" by giving them deadly injections using hypodermic needles. Then Hitler ordered the doctors to experiment with gassing the children instead.

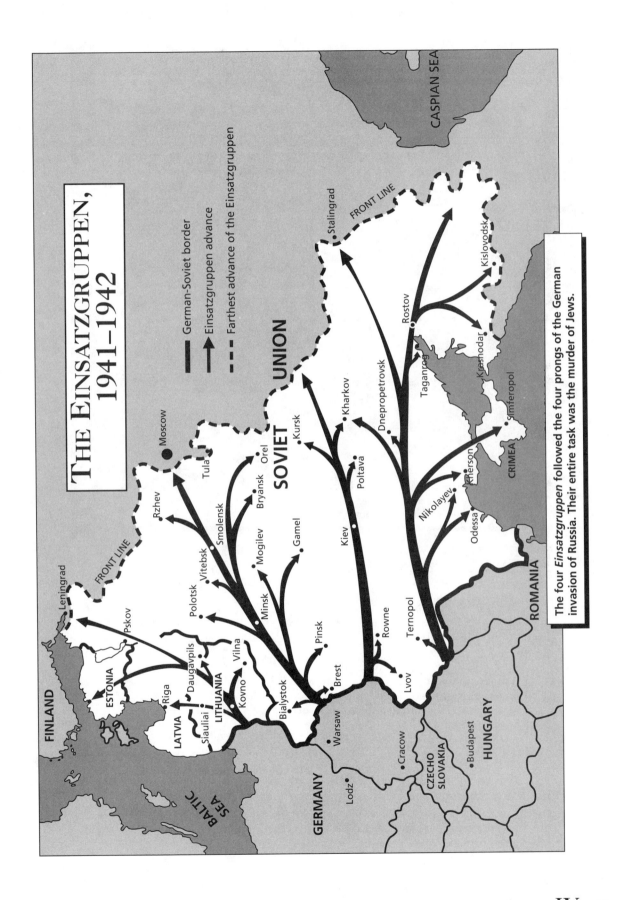

THE EINSATZGRUPPEN, 1941–1942

German-Soviet border
Einsatzgruppen advance
Farthest advance of the Einsatzgruppen

The four *Einsatzgruppen* followed the four prongs of the German invasion of Russia. Their entire task was the murder of Jews.

SOVIET UNION

FINLAND

BALTIC SEA

CASPIAN SEA

FRONT LINE

Leningrad
Pskov
ESTONIA
Riga
Daugavpils
LATVIA
Siauliai
LITHUANIA
Kovno
Vilna
Bialystok
Brest
Warsaw
GERMANY
Lodz
Cracow
CZECHO-SLOVAKIA
Budapest
HUNGARY
ROMANIA

Moscow
Rzhev
Tula
Polotsk
Vitebsk
Smolensk
Minsk
Pinsk
Mogilev
Bryansk
Orel
Gamel
Kursk
Kiev
Poltava
Kharkov
Dnepropetrovsk
Ternopol
Rowne
Lvov
Nikolayev
Odessa
Kherson
CRIMEA
Simferopol
Krashodar
Kislovodsk
Rostov
Taganrog
Stalingrad
FRONT LINE

Jews were forced to undress. Soldiers chatted in their heavy over-coats while waiting to commit the murders.

In 1941, the protests of the German people and church officials forced Hitler to close down the euthanasia program. He ordered the killing stopped, but he told his doctor friends that once the war was won, the euthanasia program would be started again.

Meanwhile, the doctors found themselves busy with another, even larger, program. Many years before, in his book *Mein Kampf*, Hitler wrote:

> If at the beginning of, or during, the war 12,000 or 15,000 of these Jewish corrupters of the people had been plunged into an asphyxiating gas. . . the sacrifice of millions of soldiers would not have been in vain.
>
> Adolf Hitler, *Mein Kampf*, p. 772

It was not too surprising that Heydrich and Eichmann decided to use the methods of the euthanasia program against Jews. In 1941 Eichmann and the doctors who had experimented with gas discussed using gas on large numbers of Jews. Following this meeting, Eichmann issued orders to build the death camps.

The First Death Camps

Experiments proved that using diesel trucks to murder Jews was both inexpensive and efficient. In the western Polish town of Kalisz, a large black truck drove up to the Jewish old age home and took a load of Jews away. Several times that weekend, the truck returned, until all the Jews of the old age home had been removed. The Jewish community demanded to know where the old people had been taken, but the Nazis only answered that they had been "relocated." Witnesses who saw the truck, however, noticed that a special pipe connected the truck's exhaust with the rear compartment, and soon the truth was known. The truck had driven until all its passengers had died of lethal carbon monoxide gas. Then the corpses had been burned or buried in a forest, which is why the Nazis had stopped traffic from leaving the city during that whole weekend. The Jewish aged of Kalisz would never return.

At the camps at Belzec, Sobibor, and Treblinka airtight buildings were constructed connected to large turbine engines that pumped out carbon monoxide gas. Then the roundups began. In the ghettos and in the cities of western Europe, Jews were gathered together for "relocation." In the words of an eyewitness:

> The following morning, a little before seven, there was an announcement: "The first train will arrive in ten minutes!" A few minutes later a train arrived from Lemberg: 45 cars with more than 6,000 people. Two hundred Ukrainians... flung open the doors and drove the Jews out of the cars with leather whips. A loudspeaker gave instructions: "Strip, even artificial limbs and glasses. Hand all money and valuables in at the 'valuables window'."
>
> Then the march began. Barbed wire on both sides, in the rear two dozen Ukrainians with rifles. . . . A tall SS man in the corner called to the unfortunates [saying,] "Nothing is going to hurt you! Just breathe deep and it will strengthen your lungs. . . ." They climbed little wooden stairs and entered the death chambers without resistance. . . . The doors closed. . . . [They] tried to start the motor. It wouldn't start!. . . 70 minutes, and the Diesel still would not start! The people were waiting in the gas chambers. You could hear them weeping. . . . The Diesel started after 2 hours and 49 minutes. . . . All were dead after thirty-two minutes! Jewish workers on the other side opened the wooden doors. They had been promised their lives in return for doing this horrible work, plus a small percentage of the money and valuables collected. The people were still standing, like columns of stone, with no room to fall or lean. Even in death you could tell the families, all holding hands. . . . Dentists knocked out gold teeth. . . . They told me that they poured Diesel oil over the bodies and burned them on railroad ties to make them disappear.
>
> Kurt Gerstein, Nuremberg Trial Document PS 1553.

The total number of victims at Belzec was close to 600,000. At Sobibor, it was 250,000. At Treblinka, it was more than 750,000; and at Chelmno, it was more than 300,000. The vast majority of these victims were Polish Jews.

Auschwitz-Birkenau

The largest concentration and death camp was at Auschwitz. It was so huge that it was sometimes called "Auschwitz city." A more deadly form of gas was used there. The company that made it specialized in making poisons for rats and pesticides for insects. It produced the lethal gas, "Zyklon B," for the extermination of insects. Now the gas was used for murdering human beings. The program of rounding up Jews to send them to Auschwitz began slowly, but after Heydrich's death in May 1942, Eichmann speeded up the transports. In Heydrich's honor, the project was named Operation Reinhard.

Transport trains filled with Hungarian Jews arrive at Auschwitz.

By 1942 the camp population was at least 150,000, and 3,000 SS men acted as guards. Auschwitz was divided into three main camps and dozens of branch camps. From that summer on, as many as four trains a day from all corners of Europe arrived at the camp. In addition to the gas chambers, four crematories with 46 ovens were built. Nearly two million people were murdered in Auschwitz and its death camp, called Birkenau, sometimes 12,000 to 15,000 in a single day.

As the trains arrived, some Jews were sent to labor camp and others were immediately sent to their deaths. This process was called "the Selection."

> The deportees move little by little toward the end of the platform. Two SS men stand in the center of the platform, one of them a medical officer. The deportees pass in front of him. With his thumb or a cane the officer sends them to the right or left. In this way two columns collect at both ends of the platform. The one on the left includes men between twenty and forty-five who have a more or less healthy appearance. . . . A few young women are also put into this column.
>
> The column on the right includes the older men, the aged, most of the women, children, and the sick. Families try to get back

together again. Sometimes the SS officer picks out those who are young and physically fit from the family. More rarely these are allowed to stay with their family in the right-hand column.

The women in the column on the left are marched off into the neighboring camp; the men are piled one on the other into trucks and trailers which then drive off. The prisoners in the right-hand column are loaded on trucks.

Robert Waitz in Poliakov, *Harvest of Hate*, p. 204.

The people in the right-hand column were marched off or sent by truck to the gas chambers. Rudolf Hess, the commandant of Auschwitz, was especially proud that the victims were usually unaware of their fate until the doors of the gas chambers were sealed tight. The Jews were told that they were going to take a shower to be disinfected. They left their clothing in "dressing rooms" on numbered hooks, and they were told to remember their numbers. They were given bars of soap. The gas chambers even had shower heads extending from the walls on all four sides. In most cases, this trick worked very well. An SS man dropped cans of Zyklon B through special windows in the roof which were then sealed shut.

Eyeglasses, combs, wedding rings—all valuables—were collected from the dead bodies before they were sent to the ovens.

Corpses, ready to be transported to the ovens. This photograph was taken by one of the first American soldiers to reach the camp at Buchenwald.

The whole process of death lasted no more than three to five minutes. Hair was shaved off the bodies of the women. Jewelry and gold teeth were removed from all bodies. Then the bodies were carted to the ovens. Incineration took another half hour. The ashes were removed and dumped into a ditch or into the nearby river.

Those Who Knew

Only a few dozen Germans had to be present at the deaths. But in total there were hundreds of thousands of eyewitnesses, including railroad workers, concentration camp guards, SS groups housed in and around Auschwitz, and German workers who supervised the Jews kept alive to do slave labor. People in the nearby town seldom spoke of it, but the special "industry" of Auschwitz was well-known to them.

Slowly, the press and radio broke the news, too. In May 1944, a newspaper in Danzig reported:

> The Jewish population of Poland has been neutralized,
> and the same may be said right now for Hungary. By this action
> five million Jews have been eliminated in these
> two countries.
>
> *Danziger Verposten*, May 13, 1944.

There were few reports inside of Germany. Many Germans did not know what was happening at all, but the truth could be guessed by others. Though most of the Nazis spoke of "evacuation" instead of "extermination," and "relocation" instead of "transport to the death camps," they sometimes let the truth slip out, even in public. In October 1943 Himmler addressed a small group of SS chiefs, saying:

> I should also like to talk very frankly to you about a very important subject. We can discuss it quite frankly among ourselves. . . . I should like to talk about the evacuation of the Jews, about the extermination of the Jewish people. . . . Most of you know what it is like to see a pile of 100 corpses. . . .
>
> This is a glorious page in our history, never before, never again to be written.
>
> Heinrich Himmler in Dawidowicz,
> *A Holocaust Reader*, pp. 132-133.

After Jews were murdered in the gas chambers, their bodies were carted to ovens to be burned to ashes.

REVIEW | ISSUES

■ This chapter ends the first unit of our study of the Holocaust. The photographs, documents, and testimonies in this section present a basic understanding of how six million Jews were murdered. It is not an easy thing to read even these few quotations or view even these few photographs. Yet they are not even one percent of the available material. Historians have been working with the documents of the Holocaust for the past fifty years, and many official government papers, trial transcripts, eyewitness accounts, memoirs, and diaries still exist that have never been studied.

■ A great number of questions remain. Who were the murderers? How did they rise to power? How could whole nations turn evil? Did no one try to help the Jews? Were there no good people in Europe? Why did other Jews not rescue the Jews of Europe and Russia? How did the Jews of the Holocaust resist? Were they ever successful in their resistance? How can Jews still believe in a God who is fair and compassionate? How did the Holocaust end? What happened to the survivors of the Holocaust?

■ Many historians believe that the Nazi plan for the destruction of the Jewish people was worked out on January 20, 1942, in a Berlin suburb called Wannsee. A nearly complete record of this meeting was made—complete, that is, up to the moment when Heydrich asked the top Nazi officials for their suggestions. The official record says, "Finally there was a discussion of the various types of solution possibilities."

1. Why would such careful notes be taken of the rest of the meeting and not of the final discussion?

■ The Nazis took care to avoid the use of words such as "extermination," "killing," and "destruction."

2. If the destruction of the Jewish people was (as Himmler said), "a glorious page in [Nazi] history," why did they avoid speaking about the large number of Jews they were destroying?

■ Review the materials about the *Einsatzgruppen*. These individuals were killing thousands of Jews each day, while at the same time their leader showed concern for their fatigued troops.

3. Were the *Einsatzgruppen* troops soldiers or criminals?

UNIT TWO

THE WORLD
AND THE JEWS

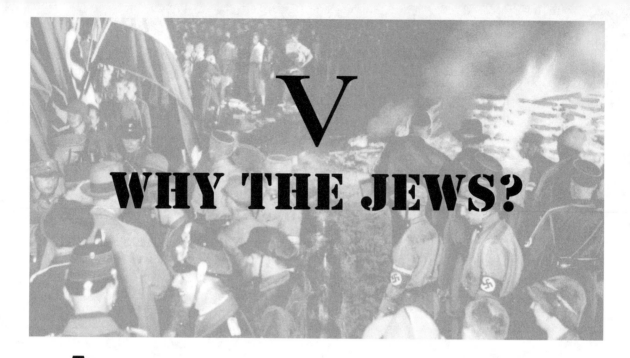

V
WHY THE JEWS?

Adolf Hitler did not invent prejudice. Prejudice has always existed. The word *prejudice* comes from Latin—the root is *judicium* ("judgment") and the prefix is *prae-* ("before"). *Webster's New World Dictionary* defines *prejudice,* "to judge before knowing." We can be prejudiced about anything, but often we use the word in a special way to speak of "suspicion, intolerance, or the traditional hatred of other races, creeds, religions, occupations, etc."

Although Hitler did not invent prejudice, he was himself a bigot, a person filled with prejudice. He hated Communists, the handicapped, gypsies, and many other human groups. Above all, he hated the Jews. He preached his prejudices to the Nazi Party and found that prejudice—especially hatred of the Jews—made him more popular. Prejudice against the Jews was common in Europe.

The Beginnings of Anti-Semitism

Jews had lived in European countries for many centuries. Nevertheless, they were considered strangers because they followed their own culture—the Torah, Jewish law, Jewish courts, Jewish education, rabbis, cantors, *kashrut*, and Jewish holidays. Their religion centered on the synagogue with its Hebrew prayers. They tended to live close together instead of spreading out among non-Jews. And they helped one another through the Jewish community, hardly ever relying on their non-Jewish neighbors for support.

In Europe, they were a minority in the lands of others. Jewish holiday practices and everyday Jewish customs seemed strange to non-Jews, even suspicious. When local laws and Jewish laws were in conflict, Jews generally chose loyalty to Judaism, even if doing so meant moving on to a new country. The Jews were strangers living according to strange laws in strange lands.

Because Jews were "different," non-Jews did not trust them. They were suspicious of Jews. They considered Jews outsiders, potential enemies, a threat. Their distrust often grew into suspicion, then superstition, then downright hatred. Anti-Jewish prejudice was a part of European Jewish life for nearly all of the last two thousand years.

For example, it was rumored that Judaism required evil acts against non-Jews. The worst rumor was called the "blood libel"—that Jews were required to kill non-Jews in order to use their blood in baking *matzot*. The idea of the blood libel goes back to ancient times. It was reported as fact by a Roman historian named Apion:

> The practice was repeated annually at a fixed season. [Jews] would kidnap a Greek foreigner, fatten him up for a year, and then convey him to a wood, where they slew him, sacrificed his body with their customary ritual, partook of his flesh, and. . . swore an oath of hostility to the Greeks. The remains of the victim were thrown into a pit.
>
> Apion (in Josephus, *Against Apion*, II, 8) cited in Flannery, *The Anguish of the Jews*, pp. 13-14.

AGE OF EUROPEAN JEWISH COMMUNITIES IN 1939

NORWAY 90 Years
ESTONIA 600 Years
North Sea
DENMARK 300 Years
LATVIA 400 Years
HOLLAND 800 Years
LITHUANIA 600 Years
BELGIUM 700 Years
RUSSIA 550 Years
GERMANY 1,600 Years
POLAND 850 Years
UKRAINE 825 Years
LUXEMBOURG 650 Years
CZECHOSLOVAKIA 1,000 Years
CRIMEA 1,900 Years
FRANCE 1,950 Years
HUNGARY 1,900 Years
AUSTRIA 1,000 Years
RUMANIA 1,800 Years
YUGOSLAVIA 1,000 YEARS
ITALY 2,100 YEARS
GREECE 2,250 Years
Black Sea
TURKEY

Jews lived throughout Europe for two thousand years—constantly facing anti-Jewish sentiment.

Jews were also accused of poisoning local water, causing diseases among non-Jews, practicing witchcraft or sorcery, and so on. Nearly all of these accusations were also made against Christians in the early days of Christianity. Later, Christians made them against the Jews. They are as obviously false about one group as about the other—but they show how fear and suspicion lead to superstition and hatred.

From time to time, a few European Jews returned to the Holy Land, hoping to escape prejudice. But the Jews were no longer a majority in the Holy Land either. It was no longer ruled by Jews, and its rulers—whether Roman, Muslim, or Christian—were often cruel.

European Jews could not be like the peoples they lived among without giving up Judaism. And even giving up Judaism was not always enough. Those who tried to blend into the majority culture found that they were never fully accepted. After converting, they were called "disloyal Jews." Some tried to "acculturate"—to take on local language and customs. And sometimes this worked. But for most Jews, through the course of two thousand years, being Jewish meant facing suspicion and hatred.

Anti-Jewish Policies of the Church

The greatest enemy of the Jews in ancient times was Rome. Yet the government of Rome was never officially anti-Jewish. True, Roman emperors sometimes outlawed Jewish practices in Judea. Yet, even when Jewish religion was outlawed in Judea, Jews in Rome and in other cities of the Roman empire were treated as full citizens and allowed to worship as they chose.

It was the rise of Christianity which placed the Jews in real danger. Most Jews rejected Christianity. Early Christians believed that they were Jews and that Christianity was only a new Jewish movement. Christians called themselves the "new Israel" or the "true Israel." In the early years of Christianity, Jews excommunicated Christians from the Jewish people. Christians accused the Jews—and not the Romans—of killing Jesus, the Christ or "messiah." The struggle grew as Christianity, especially the Catholic church, became more and more powerful.

Despite the fact that Jesus had been a Jew, many church officials—especially the less-educated local priests—taught hatred of the Jews. Throughout the Middle Ages, the church issued official anti-Jewish decrees. Later, in the twentieth century, the Nazis would follow the example the church had set.

In the year 306, the church forbade Christians from eating with Jews. On December 30, 1939, Germany passed a law barring Jews from railroad dining cars.

In the year 309, the church forbade marriage between Jews and Christians. On September 15, 1935, Germany passed the Law for the Protection of German Blood and Honor, forbidding Jews from marrying non-Jews.

In 681 the church publicly burned the Talmud and other Jewish books. The Nazis publicly burned Jewish books on May 10, 1933.

The church adopted an idea from the Muslim ruler Caliph Omar II (634-44). Omar ordered Christians to wear blue belts and Jews to wear yellow belts. In 1215, the church ordered Jews to wear special badges on their clothing. On September 1, 1941, Germany ordered that Jews wear yellow stars.

In 1267, the church decreed that Jews must live in special Jewish sections or ghettos (the word "ghetto" was first used in Venice, Italy, around 1516). On September 21, 1939, the Nazis ordered the building of ghettos to cage the Jews.

Roman coin celebrating victory in the War against Judea. The legend reads "Judea is Captive." A Roman soldier stands proudly over a weeping woman, who represents the Jewish people. The palm tree was an ancient Jewish symbol for the Land of Israel.

Anti-Jewish Policies of the States

After Rome accepted Christianity as a national religion, anti-Jewish practices and beliefs slowly became official state policies. The Nazis later adopted many of their anti-Jewish laws from these state policies of the Middle Ages.

In fourteenth-century Germany, the state declared that the property of Jews slain in a German city became public property. On July 1, 1943, the Reich Citizenship Law passed by the German government ordered that the property of a dead Jew became the property of the state.

In Nuremberg, in the fourteenth century, the state declared that if a Christian owed a debt to a Jew, the state could collect and keep it. The Reich Citizenship Law of 1943 declared the same thing.

In France in the eighteenth century and Germany in the nineteenth century, Jews were forced to carry special documents or passports marking them as Jews. On October 5, 1938, Germany passed a decree providing for special Jewish identification cards.

In Germany in the seventeenth century, the state declared that Jewish houses had to be marked, Jews could shop only during certain hours, and Jews could visit only certain places. On September 1, 1941, Germany declared certain places off-limits to Jews. On April 17, 1942, Germany declared that Jewish apartments had to be marked.

Nazi-organized public burning of Jewish books held on May 10, 1933.

Torture and Death

Anti-Jewish laws of the church and state are only one piece of the story. The long history of Jewish-Christian relations is also riddled with active persecutions of the Jews. Jews lived in the lands now called Germany for over sixteen hundred years. The first Jews in the land came as traders following the Roman legions. Wherever the traders settled, more Jews joined them.

In the Middle Ages, the Crusaders took a vow to destroy all heretics. Like the Muslims who held the Holy Land, Jews were considered heretics. Therefore, as

The Bull of Pope Julius (May 29, 1554)—an edict calling on Christians to burn the Talmud.

the Crusader armies marched across Europe on their way to Palestine, they stopped to murder (and loot) whole Jewish communities.

> The massacre of [the Jews of] Worms, on May 18, 1098, was followed... by a massacre of the Jews who had escaped to the Bishop's Palace and refused baptism.... On the 25th of Iyar, the terror descended upon those who were residing in the Bishop's Palace. The enemies killed them as they had killed the others, and slew them with the edge of the sword.... Commending their souls to the Lord, [the Jews] cried: "Hear Israel, the Lord our God, the Lord is one." Their enemies unclothed them and dragged them away, sparing no person except for a few who had accepted baptism. The numbers of those killed on those two days was eight hundred.

> Solomon Bar Simeon in
International Anthology on Racism and Anti-Semitism, p. 92.

Massacre of Jews in a Medieval town.

The ancient false accusation of blood libel continued to surface from time to time. From the twelfth to the twentieth century, Christians placed Jews and Jewish communities on trial for ritual murder over 150 times! In nearly every case, Jews were tortured and put to death. The Nazis repeated the rumors of blood libel. On May 1, 1939, the entire issue of the Nazi newspaper *Der Sturmer* was dedicated to the blood libel. The cover illustration, showing Jews murdering an Aryan child for his blood, was a drawing made in the Middle Ages. A Nazi scholar wrote:

> For our generation which currently is engaged in the severest struggle with this world pest in view of the Jewish ritual murders which ultimately sought to represent symbolically the annihilation of the non-Jewish world, there is only one possible conclusion: Spiritual and physical annihilation of the hereditary Jewish criminality.

> Helmut Schlamm in Sherwin & Ament,
Encountering the Holocaust, p. 31.

Front page of the May 1, 1939, issue of *Der Sturmer*.
The headline says, "Ritual Murder." The bottom line
reads, "The Jews are our Misfortune."

Jews were likewise accused of other religious crimes. In 1243, in
Berlitz (a city near Berlin), Jews were arrested for "desecrating the host."
The host is a *matzah*-like wafer. According to the Catholic teaching of
transubstantiation, the host becomes the flesh and wine becomes the
blood of Jesus during communion ceremonies. The Jews of Berlitz were
accused of torturing a wafer to bring Jesus to life so that they could kill
him again. As strange as this sounds, the entire Jewish community of
Berlitz was found guilty and burned alive. In Prague in 1389, the Jews
were charged with attacking a monk carrying a wafer. Three thousand
Jews were murdered.

Even after the church split into Catholics and Protestants, anti-Jewish teachings continued. Martin Luther (1483-1546), the respected leader
of the Protestant Reformation, at first tried to convert the Jews to his
new form of Christianity. When the Jews refused to convert, Luther considered them "children of the devil." He painted an ugly picture in his
book *About the Jews and Their Lies*.

Herewith you readily see how they understand and obey the fifth commandment of God, namely, that they are thirsty bloodhounds, and murderers of all Christendom... and indeed they were often burned to death upon the accusation that they had poisoned water and wells, stolen children, and torn and hacked them apart, in order to cool their temper secretly with Christian blood.... Yes, they hold us Christians captive in our country.... Then they curse our Lord.... They could not have had in Jerusalem under David and Solomon such fine days as they now have on ours—which they rob and steal daily.

Martin Luther,
Von den Juden, pp. diii3; e2.

The title page from Martin Luther's 1543 pamphlet, *About the Jews and Their Lies*.

The Nazis despised all religion, including Christianity, but they honored Luther by printing new editions of his anti-Jewish writings.

From the Enlightenment

Through the years, the Jewish community of Germany grew. Nearly 100,000 Jews served in the German army in World War I (some 12,000 were killed in the fighting). By the late 1920s more than half a million Jews lived in Germany, about a third of them in the capital city Berlin.

The Jews of modern Germany trusted in the high ideals of the German Enlightenment. The teachers of the Enlightenment used human reason to study the world. They rejected superstitions, and they accepted the work of Jewish thinkers. From the days of the Enlightenment on, the condition of Germany's Jews improved. They became full citizens in almost every sense of the word.

The Jews reacted to their new freedoms in different ways. Some converted to Christianity. Some simply stopped thinking of themselves as Jews, believing that it was enough to be a good human being in this enlightened world. Most remained Jews. Very few Jews paid attention to the rumblings of a new anti-Semitism on the rise.

Most Jews paid little notice as the German people fell in love with the operas of Richard Wagner. In his operas, Wagner celebrated the German race as the greatest race on earth. He painted a picture of Germany

Yom Kippur service for German Jewish troops in Brussels, 1915.

rising to rule the world. Like other Germans, the Jews enjoyed the operas of Wagner. They ignored Wagner's message. Richard Wagner, however, made no secret of his attitude toward Jews. In 1881 he wrote: "It is an established fact that I consider the Jewish race to be the born enemy of true mankind and of everything that is noble." Wagner was a clue to what was coming.

Modern Anti-Semitism

The new anti-Semitism growing in Germany was far different from the anti-Jewish beliefs of the church. Through the centuries the church put many Jews to death—through the Crusades, the Inquisition, and pogroms. But the church always thought of the Jews as potential converts. Jews could be saved by changing their inner beliefs and accepting Jesus and the church. The new anti-Semites saw the Jews only as enemies. The new anti-Semites believed that the Jews were members of the Semitic race—different from, less human than members of the Aryan race. Jews could not change their race, just as the leopard could not change its spots. Racist anti-Semites compared the Jews to a spreading disease.

A Nazi beer coaster. The legend reads, "Whoever buys from a Jew is a traitor to his people." The portrait is typical of Nazi anti–Semitic cartoons

Like Wagner, Hitler was a follower of the new anti-Semites. He believed in the idea of racism. "Whoever wants to understand Nazi Germany must know Wagner," Hitler said. "At every stage of my life, I come back to Richard Wagner." Hitler encouraged the scientists in Nazi Germany to study the Jews as a race and to prove scientifically that the Jewish race was inferior.

Studies of race had been popular since the end of the nineteenth century. German scientists had studied black tribes in Africa and primitive tribes in other lands. They believed that whites were superior, especially Aryan whites, people whose ancestors came from the north of Europe. They believed that "progress" meant that primitive tribes would try to catch up with the whites. But, since whites would continue to "progress" too, the more primitive peoples would never be able to actually catch up.

Hitler's "scientists" gave racism a new twist. It was popular belief that the "purest" race would eventually rule the world. In order to make Aryans the purest race, the "inferior" Jews had to be removed from Germany. This process was given the name "racial hygiene." In 1933, shortly after Hitler rose to power, a conference of "racial biologists" declared that

The significance of racial hygiene in Germany has for the first time been made evident to all enlightened Germans by the work of Adolf Hitler, and it is thanks to him that the dream we have cherished for more than thirty years of seeing racial hygiene converted into action has become a reality.

German Society for Racial Hygiene in Sherwin & Ament,
Encountering the Holocaust, p. 41.

Under Hitler, departments of "Racial Anthropology," "Political Biology," and "Racial Science" were established in German universities. "Jewish" science—any theory taught by a Jewish scientist—was attacked. For example, the scientific theories of Albert Einstein were rejected by the new German scientists on the grounds that Einstein had been too influenced by his Jewish background. German science became anti-Semitic science.

Many leading German scientists and philosophers agreed that the Jewish race was inferior. Under Hitler, those who did not agree lost their positions in the universities and their jobs in the government. Racial theories became scientific "truth." Government scientists created programs to carry out the ideals of the new racist anti-Semitism. One government expert wrote:

> First of all, we have the negative side of our work which translated into race technique means: extinction. . . . Let us not bother with old false humanitarian ideas. There is in truth only one humane idea, that is: furthering the good, eliminating the bad. The will of nature is the will of God.
>
> Cited in Sherwin & Ament, *Encountering the Holocaust*, p. 43.

Young people viewing a German anti-Semitic exhibit. One line reads: "The Jews are our misfortune."

REVIEW | ISSUES

■ Adolf Hitler did not invent hatred of Jews. The Jews were already singled out by centuries of anti-Jewish teaching and policy. Both the Church—Catholic and Protestant—and the German governments before Hitler's time had taught hatred and distrust of the Jews. By the time of Hitler, the Jewish people were a well-established enemy of state and religion.

■ Having inherited the anti-Jewish traditions of Germany, Hitler encouraged the new "scientific" anti-Semitism that appeared at the beginning of the twentieth century. He read the works of anti-Jewish scientists, listened to the words and music of men like Wagner, and encouraged the study of the inferiority of the Jewish race. Anti-Semitism was tied to "progress." Anti-Semitism became scientific "truth."

■ Gordon Allport, in his book *On the Nature of Prejudice*, points out that "a prejudiced person will almost certainly claim that he has sufficient warrant for his views [but]. . . any negative judgment of these groups must be based on characteristics that an individual has assumed that all members of an ethnic group possesses. These generalities are known as *stereotypes*."

1. What stereotypes did Europeans form of the Jews? Are all stereotypes harmful?

2. How did the teachings and policies of the church provide a basis for Nazi anti-Semitism? How did the laws of pre–Nazi Germany provide a basis for Nazi anti-Jewish laws?

3. Have you ever encountered anti-Semitism personally? How was it expressed, in idea or in action? How did you respond? How did you feel about the incident?

4. What is the difference between the anti-Jewish beliefs and actions of the church and the anti-Semitic beliefs and actions of the Nazis?

■ Looking closely at the illustrations for this chapter you will find three distinct images of the Jew—Roman, medieval, and Nazi.

5. Discuss the differences in these images: Which is the most sympathetic? Which is the least sympathetic?

6. What does each image tell us about the attitudes of the culture from which it came?

VI
THE NAZI RISE TO POWER

The great war raged from 1914 to 1918. The Allies—France, Great Britain, the United States, and Russia—called it "the war to end all wars." Today we call it World War I. When it was over, the Allies met in Versailles, France, to write a peace treaty. In 1919, they "allowed" the Central Powers—led by Germany—to sign it. The treaty contained more than 700 directives. Germany was not allowed to change even one.

The Treaty of Versailles forced Germany to admit guilt for starting the war. Germany had to give up nearly 10 percent of its land—some of its richest territory. Germany promised never again to raise a large army. And Germany promised to pay enormous sums of money to the Allies. Germany was defeated and powerless.

The people of Germany felt betrayed. The treaty hurt their pride. Most Germans were proud of their army and most believed the Allies had started the war. Most Germans lost money and property in the war. The large taxes needed to repay the Allies would make them poorer still. The Weimar Republic, the new German government, was shaky and weak, unable to raise money and unable to pay its national debts. In the end, the Treaty of Versailles did not lead to peace, as the Allies planned. Instead, it was part of a long chain of events that led to a second world war.

The Rise of Hitler

Adolf Hitler was born in Braunau am Inn, Austria, on April 20, 1889. His father, Alois, was a customs official. Alois was very strict; he would often beat Adolf. Hitler cared more for his mother, Klara. Adolf was sent to high school, but he quit at the age of fifteen. He wanted to be an artist.

By the time Hitler was twenty, both of his parents had died, and he had moved to Vienna. For a while, he lived on his orphan's pension. He applied to the Vienna Academy of Fine Arts to study painting, but he was turned down. When his pension money ran out, he painted postcards and sold them on street corners. He often ate in charity soup kitchens. He later wrote that his years in Vienna were important for only one reason: "I had ceased to be a weak-kneed cosmopolitan and became an anti-Semite."

> Once, as I was strolling through the Inner City, I suddenly encountered an apparition in a black caftan and black hair locks. Is this a Jew? was my first thought. . . . Is this a German? I bought the first anti-Semitic pamphlets of my life. . . . Wherever I went, I began to see Jews, and the more I saw, the more sharply they became distinguished in my eyes from the rest of humanity. . . . Among them was a great movement[:] this was the *Zionists*. It looked, to be sure, as though only a part of the Jews approved this viewpoint [but] the so-called liberal Jews did not reject Zionists as non-Jews. . . . Intrinsically, they remained unalterably of one piece.
>
> Adolf Hitler, *Mein Kampf*, p. 85.

In Vienna, Hitler read anti-Semitic newspapers and journals. He studied a newsletter called the *Ostara*—a strange mixture of anti-Semitism, false science regarding the Aryan master race, and mystic

The Allies force Germany to sign the Treaty of Versailles in the Hall of Mirrors. Detail from a painting by Sir William Orpen.

topics like the meaning and origin of the swastika. Other anti-Semitic writings spoke of racial purity and the need for a strong *fuhrer* ("leader") for the Aryan *volk*, the German people.

In Vienna, Hitler watched as the mayor, Karl Lueger, used anti-Semitism as a political tool. The people of Vienna loved Lueger, voting for him in election after election. Lueger's anti-Semitism was not serious enough for Hitler. Lueger hated Jews only for religious reasons. If a Jew converted, Lueger no longer hated him. As Hitler said, "a splash of baptismal water could always save the business and the Jew at the same time." Hitler's own anti-Semitism was based not on religion, but on race—a Jew could not escape it by converting.

In May 1913, Hitler moved to Munich. He was still a loner. He continued peddling his mediocre sketches and drawings. He continued studying racism, too, but he also began lecturing in taverns and beer halls among other anti-Semites. On August 1, 1914, Germany declared war. Hitler immediately joined the army. He was sent to France, where he was wounded in the fighting. After receiving the Iron Cross, Second Class, for valor, he returned to the front as a lance corporal. In October 1918, he was caught in a British gas attack. This time he received the Iron Cross, First Class. In the hospital, at the war's end, Hitler decided to enter politics.

The Nazi Party

In 1919, Hitler took a job as "education officer" for the District Army Command—his first real job. He prepared reports on the many political groups around Munich. This assignment brought him to a meeting of the German Workers' Party. This small group talked mostly about how much better things were before the war. Hitler realized that they had no leader. He joined the group, forced them to accept a new political program, and changed the group's name to the National Socialist German Workers' (Nazi) Party.

In November 1920, Hitler made his first public speech. Much to his own surprise, Hitler discovered that he was a captivating speaker. He began by speaking low and slow, finishing in a high-pitched furious torrent of words. He soon attracted large audiences. Always he spoke of Germany's defeat in the war, blaming the Jews for "stabbing Germany in the back." A summary of one speech reports that Hitler concluded: "We will carry on the struggle until the last Jew is removed from the German Reich." Nazi Party membership grew.

The Munich Putsch

Hitler used members and their money to improve the Nazi Party. Armbands and banners were created—a red background that stood for blood, a white circle that stood for nationalism, and the twisted cross that stood for the Aryan struggle. Hitler trained some party members as "storm

The first Storm Troopers were trained without the use of firearms. Note the ever-present Nazi armbands.

troopers," forming a private army called the SA (*Sturmabteilung*).

On November 8, 1923, Hitler and his storm troops surrounded a meeting of government officials in a beer hall in Munich. He threatened to kill them unless they swore loyalty to his "revolution." But as soon as they were freed, they turned on Hitler and had him arrested. Crowds showed up for the trial, cheering Hitler. The court gave him the lightest possible sentence, five years with a chance for parole after six months. News of his failed "beer hall *Putsch*" spread, and Hitler's name was heard far and wide for the first time. The press recorded Hitler's statements during the trial:

> The man who is born to be a dictator is not compelled. He wills it. He is not driven forward, but impels himself. There is nothing immodest about this. . . . The man who feels called to govern a people has no right to say, "If you want me or summon me, I will cooperate." No! It is his duty to step forward.
>
> The army we have trained is growing from day to day, from hour to hour.
>
> Adolf Hitler in Foreman, *Nazism*, pp. 40-41.

Hitler served nine months before he was pardoned. In prison with him was Rudolf Hess, a member of the Nazi Party since 1920. Hess offered to put Hitler's ideas into a book. Hitler spoke, and Hess wrote. (Hess later became one of Hitler's chief deputies.) The book was called *Mein Kampf* ("My Struggle"), and from the moment it was printed it became the handbook of the Nazi Party. In it, Hitler spoke out on anti-Semitism, the "Jewish plot," racism, the Aryan nation, and *lebensraum*—the idea that Aryans need more land for "living space."

Released from prison, Hitler was forbidden to make public speeches. Hitler became the only *fuhrer* ("leader") of the Nazis. He turned his energies to creating a state within a state.

A billboard advertises Hitler's Nazi handbook, *Mein Kampf.* The message reads, "I read endlessly and thoroughly. Within a few years, I had created a base of knowledge that I still tap today."

The SA, led by Hitler's close friend Ernst Rohm, was becoming a problem for Hitler. The Storm Troopers were difficult to control. In 1925 Hitler set up a smaller army, the *Schutzstaffel* or SS. At first there were only 280 SS men, led by another of Hitler's friends, Heinrich Himmler. By 1934, the SS numbered 250,000 members. It was better organized, and more dangerous, than the far larger SA.

Within the Nazi Party, he set up departments of agriculture, justice, labor, foreign affairs, and so on. The Nazi Party became a mirror of the German government, ready to replace that government. Hitler waited for the right moment.

The Great Depression

The right moment came in October 1929. In the United States, the Stock Market crashed, and the Great Depression began. Millionaires became beggars overnight. Banks closed. Middle-class people lost their savings. Companies went bankrupt. Factories and stores closed. Jobs were scarce.

During the Depression, Germans line up in the snow in front of the municipal kitchen, waiting for bread.

Germany had taken huge loans from U.S. banks to help repay the Versailles war debt. Suddenly, the banks called in the loans. The German people were worse off than before. To pay debts and taxes, many were forced to sell homes and personal belongings. Only two political parties could claim that they had known this would happen. One was the Communist Party. The other was Hitler's Nazi Party.

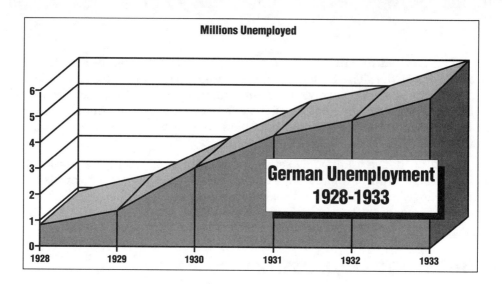

Millions Unemployed

German Unemployment 1928-1933

1928 1929 1930 1931 1932 1933

Unemployment was a major cause for the rise of the Nazi Party.

Hitler seized the moment. He crisscrossed Germany by plane, automobile, and train—making as many as three speeches a day. He promised jobs. He promised to rebuild the army. He promised to defeat the Communists. He promised to defeat the Jewish traitors who had caused all Germany's troubles. In Munich hundreds had come to hear him, now he spoke before thousands.

In 1928, the Nazis had won 800,000 votes. In 1930, they won 6.5 million votes, becoming the second largest party in Germany. They controlled more than a hundred seats in the Reichstag, the German congress. Military leaders liked Hitler's promise to rebuild the army. Business leaders hated the weak government of the present party. They liked the idea of building factories and spending money to rebuild the army. Many Germans understood that rebuilding the army would mean more jobs, too. Smaller anti-Semitic parties joined the Nazis. By the mid-1930s SA membership was nearly 500,000. Finally, on January 30, 1933, President Paul von Hindenberg called on Hitler to be the new chancellor of Germany. Hitler swore the oath of office, promising to protect the German constitution and its laws, to be fair and just to all Germans.

An End of Democracy

Even as he took the oath of office, Hitler was planning the end of the German republic. New elections were set for March 1933, and Hitler wanted to ensure that the Nazis would win a majority. The Nazis set fire to the

Reichstag building on February 28, blaming a fanatic Dutch anarchist. Hitler seized on the fire as he had the Great Depression. Arriving at the scene of the fire, Hitler swore to arrest "everyone responsible." The list had already been drawn up. Before the fire stopped smoldering, four thousand of Hitler's enemies were in prison. They were mostly Communists, plus a few journalists, doctors, and attorneys.

Next Hitler called on the president. He convinced the aging Hindenberg to sign an emergency decree "for the protection of the people and the state." This decree cancelled all individual and civil rights. It placed all power in the hands of Hitler and the Nazi Party. Germans were forbidden to express their beliefs freely, to assemble to hear political speeches (except Hitler's), or to gather in large groups. Hitler was given the right to control newspapers and radio broadcasts. The Nazis could open mail, read telegrams, listen in on telephone conversations, and search houses without warning.

With all this power, the Nazis gained 44 percent of the vote in the March elections. Hitler was still not satisfied. On March 23, the SS marched outside the opera house in which the *Reichstag* was meeting. Hitler put forward the Enabling Act, a law that would make him the only one who could propose new laws and give him the power to alter the constitution. As the *Reichstag* voted, the SS men outside chanted, "We demand the Enabling Act or there will be hell to pay!" The Enabling Act passed. Within a few months, the Nazi Party was Germany's only political party. All other parties were outlawed.

On May 10, 1933, with SA and SS men in charge, "un-German books" were piled high in Berlin and set aflame. Josef Goebbels, Hitler's Minister of Propaganda, proclaimed that "the spirit of the German people can again express itself. These flames not only illuminate the final end of an old era, they also light up the new."

A century before, the national German poet, Jewish-born Heinrich Heine, had offered a far different kind of wisdom. "Where books are burned," Heine wrote, "in the end men will burn as well."

Night of the Long Knives

As the leader of Germany, Hitler needed the support of the regular German military. He tried to join the SA to the military, but military leaders refused to accept the undisciplined Storm Troopers. Himmler warned Hitler that SA leader Rohm's power was growing, and Rohm might soon challenge Hitler himself. In the end, Hitler had little choice. He had to bring the SA under strict control. But how?

For months, Himmler and the SS trained and plotted. They chose cities in which to attack the SA, trained SS men for the attack, and drew up lists of enemies of the Nazis to execute. On the lists, only about half were leaders of the SA; the others were "unwanted" individuals. On June 29, 1934, Hitler gave the order and the purge of the SA began. The purge came to be called the Night of the Long Knives. It lasted a little more than two days. In that time, nearly 200 people—including Ernst Rohm—were put to death without trial. The power of the SA was broken forever. Two days later, Hitler's cabinet passed a one-sentence law, making the purge legal: "The measures taken on June 30, July 1 and 2 to suppress treasonable activities are legally considered to have been taken in emergency defense of the state."

Hitler had shown that he was capable of cold-blooded murder. Not only had he killed political enemies, but he had also killed many who had been his supporters since the beginning, even his close friend, Rohm. When he was through murdering, he issued a law making the murders legal. When President von Hindenberg died in August 1934, Adolf Hitler became the absolute dictator of Germany. He could say and do as he pleased.

Hitler delights Nazi Party members in the Munich Beer Cellar.

Nazi rally. The flags read "Germany awake."

Heinrich Himmler

Heinrich Himmler

Himmler was born in 1900, served in World War I, took a job in Munich, and joined the Nazi Party. He marched with Hitler in the Beer Hall Putsch, and Hitler chose him as the leader of the SS in 1929. Himmler was determined to make his SS an elite group within the Nazi Party. In the beginning, he handpicked the men, trained them carefully, suited them in ominous black uniforms, and kept strict military order in the ranks. Eventually the Third Reich became an SS state, and Himmler was given direct command of the destruction of the Jews.

Himmler, together with his assistant, Reinhard Heydrich, chose Adolf Eichmann to head the Jewish desk. He supervised the mass killings but took time out to practice his hobby—planting herb gardens. At the end of the war, he tried to escape by disguising himself as a Gestapo sergeant. The Allies recognized him and he was captured, but he committed suicide before the Nuremberg War Crimes Trials.

Reinhard Heydrich

Reinhard Heydrich

Heydrich was a man who ached for power. Many of the other Nazi leaders were genuinely afraid of him; some believed that Heydrich would one day be the next Fuhrer. It was known that he kept records on every leader, to be used for blackmail. Hitler called him "the man with the iron heart." He was tall and blond, and loved sports.

Heydrich had joined the SS after being court-martialled out of the German Navy in 1930. It was said that he once shot a mirror because he didn't like the way it made him look. He became an expert in murder and mayhem, and by 1936, he had become the head of the Gestapo, the SD (the internal security arm of the SS), and the Criminal Police. The fate of the Jews was placed in his hands in 1939. He was also named "Protector" of Bohemia and Moravia.

In 1941 Heydrich was sent to Prague, Czechoslovakia to bring it under control. He was so successful that the Czech government in exile in Britain parachuted two assassins into the country to kill him. They threw a bomb under his car on May 27, 1942. When he died, many of the Nazi leaders secretly breathed a sigh of relief.

NAZI LEADERS

Josef Goebbels

Hitler was an expert in the use of propaganda. But close at hand, he had an even greater master of the art, Josef Goebbels. Goebbels was a failed university professor when he first joined the Nazi Party in the mid–1920s. He soon became one of Hitler's most devoted followers. In the party, he found that his greatest talent was organized lying. Though he preached the virtues of the Aryan race, he was dark, short, weak, and club-footed.

Goebbels made skillful use of the radio and press, and his grand arrangements for national rallies and celebrations, together with his deep-seated anti-Semitism, created Hitler's image as the German messiah. He was constantly in Hitler's company. It was Goebbels who organized the suicides of Hitler and his wife, Eva; Goebbels, his wife, and his six children, in a Berlin bunker at the end of the war.

Josef Goebbels

Hermann Goering

Goering loved titles, prince-like luxury, and power. He was Supreme Leader of the Prussian Gestapo, an SS General, President of the *Reichstag*, Minister for Air, Commander-in-Chief of the Air Force, Marshal, and official successor to Hitler. In World War I, Goering was a highly decorated pilot. At the war's end, he was deeply disturbed by the Versailles treaty. He was an expert organizer, something he proved by transforming the mainly criminal SA into an efficient fighting force. He was also an animal lover, a patron of the arts, and a conservationist.

Early in the war, Goering's *Luftwaffe* (the German air force) was very successful, and Hitler trusted him deeply. As the *Luftwaffe* began to lose the battle for the air, Hitler began to ignore him. In the meanwhile, Goering had six palatial homes, lived on caviar and champagne, and collected art. He was captured and tried at Nuremberg, where he was sentenced to death by hanging. But he committed suicide before the hanging could take place.

Hermann Goering

Adolf Eichmann

Adolf Eichmann

From the time that he was appointed to the Jewish desk in Berlin, Eichmann devoted himself to the destruction of the Jews of Europe. He was a member of the SS and the SD. He was never a public figure in Germany, but after the war he became famous as the man who had engineered all the details of the Holocaust.

Eichmann was born in 1906 in the Rhineland. His family moved to Upper Austria, where he attended a school where Hitler had once been a student. He returned to Germany and joined the Nazi Party in 1932. From his small office, Eichmann ran the entire transport, concentration camp, and death camp process. He escaped to South America at the end of the war, but in 1960 he was captured by agents of the Israeli secret police and brought to trial in Israel in 1961. His trial brought the Holocaust to world attention, exposing much of the story of Jewish resistance, and renewing Holocaust studies around the world. He was found guilty and hanged in May 1962. His body was burned and his ashes scattered from a plane flying over the Mediterranean Sea.

July 1933. Hitler, Germany's absolute dictator, prepares to address an SA rally in the city of Dortmund

REVIEW | ISSUES

■ Hitler was a spellbinder when he spoke. But his speechmaking alone could never have brought him to power. He was a vicious anti-Semite, but anti-Semitism alone could not have brought him to power.

■ It was Hitler's skill as an organizer and the twin tragedies of world politics and the world economy that swept Hitler into the dictatorship of Germany. If only the German nation had been helped to recover after World War I; if only the Germans had not had such a long history of anti-Jewish behavior; if only the Great Depression had not brought German unemployment to six million people; if only the military and businessmen of Germany had not placed their trust in Hitler; if only the aging President von Hindenberg had been more strong-willed—if only one of these had been true, Hitler and the Nazi Party might never have come to power in Germany. Yet all of these events lined up in a row, like the earth, moon, and sun do in a total eclipse to create darkness.

■ In many ways, Vienna was like a college education for the young Hitler. In particular, he was able to study the political style of a famous anti-Semite, Karl Lueger. The difference he noted between Lueger's anti-Semitism and his own is critical for understanding the Holocaust.

1. Explain the difference between Hitler's anti-Semitism and Lueger's anti-Semitism in your own words.

2. Was Adolf Hitler a product of his time, a master criminal, or a brilliant madman? Use the information in the chapter to support your opinion.

■ What did the Nazi leaders have in common? What differences do you notice?

■ Look up "swastika" in an encyclopedia. What is the origin of this symbol? How has it been used throughout history? How many different cultures have used it?

VII
PEOPLE WILL BELIEVE WHAT THEY ARE TOLD

Violence and fear were the main tools of the Nazis during their rise to power. But once they came to power, the Nazis forged a new state. They successfully united and organized the German people. They improved economic conditions in Germany. They entered into treaties with other nations. Hitler and the other Nazi leaders had prepared themselves to use the tools of modern government.

But all along Hitler combined these with another, extremely important tool, propaganda. "Propaganda has absolutely nothing to do with truth," said the Nazi Minister of Propaganda, Paul Josef Goebbels. Propaganda is organized, carefully designed lying. Propaganda, Hitler wrote in *Mein Kampf*, "must always be addressed to the masses [and] must confine itself to a very few points and repeat them endlessly." And Goebbels added, "Any lie, frequently repeated, will gradually gain acceptance."

Even before Hitler became dictator, Goebbels was directing Nazi propaganda in Berlin. He designed striking campaign posters, issued pamphlets, and published a weekly newspaper, *Der Angriff* ("The Attack"). When the American-made anti-war film, *All Quiet on the Western Front*, opened in Berlin, Goebbels released white mice and harmless snakes in the theater. These were small beginnings, but good practice for what would come next.

On March 13, 1933, Goebbels was made Hitler's head of propaganda for the Third Reich. He was in charge of

> all influences on the intellectual life of the nation; for public relations for state, culture, and the economy; and for the administration of all the institutions serving these purposes.
>
> Decree of March 13, 1933 cited in *The New Order*, p. 57.

Goebbels' office was in an old palace. From the palace, he selected some of the best and most highly educated young men he could find, setting up thirty-two regional offices. With Hitler's blessing, Goebbels founded a new Reich Chamber of Culture. The chamber had seven departments—literature, theater, music, film, fine arts, the press, and radio. Anyone who "produced, distributed, or sold" any kind of culture had to join one of these departments and obey the orders of the president of the chamber, Goebbels. Of course, Jews were not allowed to join, most non-Aryans were not allowed to join, and all enemies of Hitler were also excluded. Without a license to practice, Jewish artists and writers could no longer sell their work, Jewish publishers were not allowed to publish books, and Jewish producers and directors were not allowed to make films. Jewish newspapers and magazines were outlawed and no Jewish voice was heard on the radio.

Paul Josef Goebbels was not only brilliant at arranging propaganda, he was also one of the Nazis' best speakers.

The Place of Women

Propaganda was used in every quarter. Hitler wanted to build a larger nation. For that, he needed more Aryans. The masses had to change their idea of what a woman should be like. The old image of beauty—the slim woman with the hourglass shape—had to be replaced with a new image of beauty. New fashion models were chosen from women who were pleasingly plump, motherly looking. Artists were encouraged to use German mothers as models. Hitler even awarded a national medal to women who gave birth to six or more children.

In 1937, SS men were instructed not to marry blond-haired, blue-eyed women who had not earned the Reich sports medal. Goebbels sent out a press release to explain:

> Germany does not need women who can dance beautifully at five o'clock teas, but women who have given proof of their health through accomplishments in the field of sport. "The javelin and the springboard are more useful than lipstick in promoting health."
>
> Josef Goebbels in Mosse, *Nazi Culture*, p. 280.

Hitler's idea was that women look like mothers and spend their lives having children and taking care of the family. These girls from a German homemaking school were the ideal Nazi type.

The place of the Nazi woman was in the home, raising the children. Hitler told the Nazi women's organization:

> So long as we possess a healthy manly race. . . we will form no female mortar battalions and no female sharpshooter corps. For that is not equality of rights, but a lessening of the rights of women. . . .
>
> I am often told: You want to drive women out of the professions. Not at all. I wish only. . . for her to cofound her own family and to be able to have children, because by so doing she most benefits our [Aryan] folk!. . .

If today a female jurist accomplishes ever so much and next door there lives a mother with five, six, seven children, who are all healthy and well-brought-up, then I would like to say: From the standpoint of the eternal value of our people the woman who has given birth to children and raised them and who thereby has given back our people life for the future has accomplished more and does more!

Adolph Hitler in Mosse, *Nazi Culture*, p. 280.

Nazi Education

If it was important for German women to have more children, it was equally important that those children be educated by Nazi teachers. Jewish teachers were fired. Teachers who would not swear loyalty to Nazism were also dismissed. Nearly 97 percent of Germany's teachers belonged to the Nazi teachers' association.

Textbooks and readers were changed to teach Nazism in every class. Even a math problem could encourage young people to think like Nazis:

A modern bomber can carry 1,800 incendiaries. How long is the path along which it can distribute these bombs if it drops a bomb every second at a speed of 250 kilometers per hour? How far apart are the craters?

Cited in *The New Order*, p. 103.

The Nazis encouraged all boys to become members of the Hitler Youth, a movement that trained them in anti-Semitism, sports, and military behavior. Girls had a similar movement called the League of German Girls. Early readers were given an anti-Semitic reader entitled, *Don't Trust the Fox in the Green Meadow or the Jew on His Oath*. In part, it read:

Young people who call themselves real Germans join the Hitler Youth. They dedicate their lives to the Fuhrer and strive for the future. . . . You can see the Hitler Youth, proud and handsome. They are all tall and proud fellows, from the biggest to the smallest man.
They love the German Fuhrer.
They fear God in heaven.
They despise the Jews—
[Jews] are not like them.
That's why [Jews] must go.

Cited in *Teaching about the Holocaust and Genocide*, Vol 2, p. 43.

Another child's primer was called *The Poisonous Mushroom*. It was published by Julius Streicher, whose anti-Semitism was so fanatic that it even made many Nazis uncomfortable. Streicher was also the publisher of *Der Sturmer*, the anti-Semitic newspaper that had renewed the false accusation against Jews called the blood libel. *The Poisonous Mushroom* was very popular. It told the story of a young girl named Inge who was sent to keep an appointment with a Jewish doctor. Her leader in the League of German Girls warned her not to go. But there she was, nervously waiting in the doctor's office.

> Then the door opens. Inge looks up. The Jew appears. She screams. . . . Horrified she jumps up. Her eyes stare into the face of the Jewish doctor. And this face is the face of the Devil. In the middle of this devil's face is a huge crooked nose. Behind the spectacles gleam two criminal eyes. Around the thick lips plays a grin, a grin that means, "Now I have you at last, you little German girl!" And then the Jew approaches her. His fat fingers snatch at her. But now Inge has got hold of herself. Before the Jew can grab hold of her, she smacks the fat face of the Jew doctor with her hand. One jump to the door. Breathlessly Inge runs down the stairs. Breathlessly she escapes from the Jew house.

Cited in International Military Tribunal, Vol V, pp. 114-116.

Cover of the Nazi primer, *Don't Trust the Fox in the Green Meadow or the Jew on His Oath*.

Another book for young people was even more direct. Across from a picture of Streicher was a caption that read, in part, "Without a solution of the Jewish question there will be no salvation for mankind." Other Nazis might shrink at Streicher's extremist campaign of anti-Semitism. Not Hitler. The Fuhrer called it "a skillful and amusing campaign" and added, "Where does Streicher get all his ideas?"

With books like these and the intense campaign directed at German youth, it is not difficult to imagine what a discussion in a German elementary school might be like. The Hitler Youth and the League gained many members. Were all these young people anti-Semites? Were they all taken in by the Nazi propaganda? One German who joined the Hitler Youth remembers:

> There was no pressure put on me by my father or anyone else to join the Hitler Youth—I decided to join it independently simply because I wanted to be in a boys' club where I could strive towards a nationalistic ideal. The Hitler Youth had camping, hikes, and group meetings [and, after Hitler came to power,] political indoctrination. . . . I think most of the other boys joined for the same reason I did. They were looking for a place where they could get together with other boys in exciting activities. It was also a depression time and there were many. . . influences abroad which decent boys wished to escape. In any event, I don't think the political factor was the main reason boys joined. . . . We weren't fully conscious of what we were doing, but we enjoyed ourselves and also felt important.
>
> William Allen in Chartook & Spencer, *The Holocaust Years*, p. 122.

The Hitler Youth in an illustration from *Don't Trust the Fox*.

A card proving that this young German belonged to the Hitler Youth.

Newspapers, Radio, Film

Control of the German mind was the real goal of the propaganda machine. That meant controlling what people read, saw, and heard. At first, there were too many newspapers in Germany for the Nazis to control them all. So Goebbels took over the wire services that fed stories to the newspapers at home and abroad. He joined them into the German News Bureau and controlled the newspapers at their source. The Editors' Law of 1933 declared that all newspaper editors had to be officially "approved" by Goebbels' ministry. Editors were held responsible for every word in their newspapers and could lose their jobs if the ministry did not like what was printed. At daily press conferences, Goebbels and his team told reporters what to write, how it should be written, and even how large their headlines could be. After *Kristallnacht*, for example, Goebbels told reporters to make only small mention of the cost of damages and to concentrate instead on the anger of the German people toward the Jews.

How serious was Goebbels' control of the press? One example is enough: In Essen, a newspaper typesetter accidentally placed a caption intended for a carnival photograph under a photo of marching Storm Troopers. The editor and the publisher of the newspaper were arrested and sent to a concentration camp. More often, editors lost their jobs, reporters lost their licenses, or whole editions of newspapers were seized and destroyed. In a while, the newspapers were so one-sided and boring that millions of Germans stopped reading newspapers altogether.

But Goebbels could also control what was heard on the radio. The Nazis made sure that very cheap radios were available in the stores. By 1939, 70 percent of German homes had at least one radio—the highest rate of radio ownership in all of Europe. In a broadcast day of nineteen hours, nearly five hours were devoted to Nazi propaganda. The rest was news (from Goebbels' wire service), opera, folk songs, marches, and waltzes. The Nazis encouraged people to gather in small groups to listen to radio—families in their homes, workers in factories, men in the beer halls. They even mounted loudspeakers all over the country and blasted out the radio broadcasts in every sort of public area. In this pre-television era, the Nazi radio campaign literally controlled what people could hear.

A terrifying pamphlet advertises the Nazi-made, anti-Semitic movie, *Jud Suss*. The film was so horrifying that the actors asked Goebbels to send out a special press release telling the country that they themselves were not Jewish.

Goebbels was himself a great fan of the movies. He had private screening rooms built into each of his three houses and, no matter how busy his schedule, he watched at least one film each day. Among his favorites was *Gone with the Wind*. He was upset when many of the most talented movie stars, producers, and directors fled the country after the Hitler takeover, but many of them were Jewish, and others left for countries where they would not be under Nazi control. The Minister of Propaganda approved the script for every film made in Germany, gave money or tax breaks to help make films he was particularly interested in, and commissioned special documentaries to show the glories of Nazism.

One of the most dazzling documentary films ever made was *Triumph of the Will*, which glorified Hitler and the 1934 Nuremberg party rally. More than a million Germans gathered to hear the Fuhrer on this

Adolf Hitler poses with a German girl after giving her an autographed picture of himself. Through control of the newspapers and radio, Goebbels made Hitler into a superstar.

Hitler visits a farm family in East Prussia. Propaganda pictures like this portrayed Hitler as a kind and friendly leader who cared deeply about his people.

occasion. The film's director worked with 30 cameras and 120 technicians, and even helped to direct what would happen during the rally, to make it more dramatic for the cameras.

> To see the films of the Nuremberg rallies even today is to be recaptured by the hypnotic effect of thousands of men marching in perfect order, the music of the massed bands, the forest of standards and flags, the vast perspectives of the stadium, the smoking torches, the dome of searchlights. The sense of power, of force and unity was irresistible, and all converged with a mounting crescendo of excitement on the supreme moment when the Fuhrer himself made his entry.
>
> Alan Bullock in Snell, *The Nazi Revolution,* p. 6.

Cleaning Out the Library Shelves

Goebbels' chief competitor in Nazi propaganda control was Alfred Rosenberg, a close friend of Hitler, a one-time editor of the official Nazi newspaper, and a fanatical anti-Semite. Rosenberg ran an organization called the Fighting League for German Culture. The Fighting League organized book burnings throughout Germany—works by Sigmund Freud, Karl Marx, Albert Einstein, Ernest Hemingway, Thomas Mann, H. G. Wells, Maxim Gorki, and hundreds of other authors were officially approved for burning. Some of these authors were Jews, others (like Thomas Mann, the German Nobel Prize winner) had written approvingly of Jews, others were simply too liberal or too communist. Nearly 2,500 writers fled the country after the first round of book burnings. Goebbels matched Rosenberg by blacklisting more than 12,400 titles, all of which were removed from libraries and confiscated from bookstores. Using propaganda and advertising, he made *Mein Kampf* into the national best seller—nearly 6.2 million copies were sold.

Did all this propaganda fool the German people? Not altogether. One German worker joked to a foreign correspondent: "I told my wife that if I die, don't let them put it into the newspaper, because no one will believe it." Many Germans stopped trusting the news they heard or read, and they blamed the sad state of their culture on the Ministry of Propaganda.

The propaganda did succeed, however, in making many Germans believe the myth of Hitler's leadership. They loved the Fuhrer so much that many created small "Hitler corners" in their homes, shrines in which Hitler's portrait hung. During the war, it was even believed that a home with such a shrine was safe from enemy attack.

"Hitler corner" in a German home. Many Germans thought their little shrines were good luck charms. Here a devoted German girl honors Hitler by decorating the shrine with fresh flowers.

■ Not every German was a member of the Nazi Party. That was not Hitler's goal. The goal was to make every German believe in Nazi ideas and ideals. The tool for accomplishing that goal was propaganda. Albert Speer, Nazi Minister for Armaments and War Production, in his final speech at his trial after the war, summed up much of the meaning of controlling the masses through propaganda:

> Hitler's dictatorship differed in one fundamental point from all its predecessors in history. His was the first dictatorship. . . which made complete use of all technical means for the domination of its own country.
>
> Through technical devices like the radio and the loudspeaker, 80 million people were deprived of independent thought. It was thereby possible to subject them to the will of one man.
>
> Albert Speer in Snell,
> *The Nazi Revolution*, p. 7.

■ Alan Bullock, one of Hitler's biographers, said that Hitler's downfall was caused by the very propaganda that he created. Hitler came to believe that he really was capable of working miracles, that he really was historically chosen to be Germany's savior. Bullock observed, "If ever a man was destroyed by the image he had created it was Adolf Hitler."

■ Albert Speer observed that it was "the technical means"—radio, telephone, telegraph, and loudspeakers—which allowed Hitler to control the people. Others believe it was propaganda that made the difference. As Goebbels said, "Any lie, frequently repeated, will gradually gain acceptance."

1. Which of these opinions do you think is correct?

2. How could the German people know that they were being subjected to propaganda, and still come to love Hitler as the Fuhrer? (Hint: You may wish to read again the statement of William Allen describing his reasons for joining the Hitler Youth.)

■ The Talmud (*Shabbat* 55a) calls truth "the seal of God." Only truth can sustain order in the world. Lying twists language—it causes confusion. The truth is orderly—it makes sense at once.

3. This is a lovely teaching, but is it true? Can you always tell a lie from the truth?

4. What tests can you use to see if a government is lying to you?

■ Imagine yourself as an American reporter who last visited Germany in 1930, just after the Great Depression began. The year is now 1941, and you are sent to Germany again.

5. What changes do you notice? What role did the press and the media play in these changes?

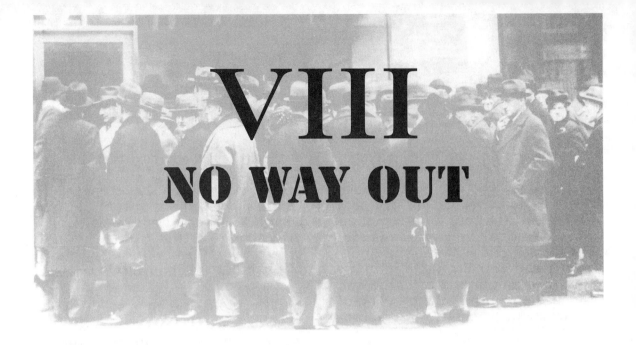

VIII
NO WAY OUT

There were more than 500,000 Jews in Germany in 1933. The great majority of them had been born and raised in Germany. The German Jews lived in Berlin (30 percent), in other large cities (40 percent), and scattered in small communities throughout the rest of the country. More than half of them owned or operated businesses.

German Jews behaved as citizens, paying normal taxes. In addition, each community paid taxes to and governed itself through an organization called a *Gemeinde*. The *Gemeinde* maintained the synagogue, Jewish education, and Jewish charities. Many Jews also belonged to the Jewish Central Association (CV). Most Jews were anti-Zionist—not wishing to support a return to the Holy Land, or not wishing to "force God's hand" by trying to create a Jewish state in the Holy Land. Some supported the idea of a Jewish homeland only as a refuge that, of course, they never expected to need. As soon as Hitler came to power in 1933, the CV declared:

> We are convinced that no one will dare to violate our constitutional rights. Every adverse attempt will find us at our post ready for resolute defense. . . . Stand by calmly.
>
> *CV Zeitung*, February 2, 1933.

Nazi laws, however, soon drove Jews from their government jobs and their professions. Thousands of Jews were suddenly without jobs. Even before *Kristallnacht*, some 400 Jewish communities disappeared or were being dissolved, as Jews moved into the larger cities looking for jobs and the protection of numbers. Before Hitler, German Jews had trusted in the logic and compassion of the German people. Looking back at the history of their own community, they saw long cycles of anti-Semitism and recovery. They were sure that Hitler was a passing phase.

Many German Jews thought of themselves as Germans who happened to be born Jewish. But Hitler's laws affected them as Jews and not

Germans. The SA and the local population suddenly turned on them just because they were Jews. Their lifelong faith in the honor of Germany was shaken. Suicide was one way out. Some 350 Jews committed suicide between 1932 and 1934. One *Gemeinde* issued a public plea:

> Under the shattering impact of the events of recent weeks, during which suicide claimed victim upon victim within our community, we turn to you. . . . *Maintain your courage and will to live, preserve your confidence in God and in yourself!*. . . Do not take the path into darkness from which there is no return.
>
> The *Gemeinde* of Colone in Dawidowicz,
> *The War Against the Jews*, p. 232.

Why Not Run?

Another, better, way out was to leave Germany. About one-third of German Jewry left before the Holocaust. Many of those who left were public figures: writers, actors, scientists, teachers, even a few prominent businessmen. But most of them did not go far. Some purposely stayed in Europe, expecting to return to Germany as soon as things calmed down. They went to places like France, Poland, Holland, and Belgium—within a few years the Holocaust caught up with them. Because immigration to Palestine was limited, only about 38,000 German Jews were able to enter Palestine between 1933 and 1938. What about America? Some did head for the United States, but U.S. immigration laws kept the numbers small.

Many German Jews felt that it was a religious duty, almost a *mitzvah*, to stay. The CV, in its newspaper of April 13, 1933, wrote, "It is our aim to preserve within Germany a German-Jewish community, unbroken financially, physically, and spiritually." One leader of the CV spoke of the German Jewish future:

> Fear? We have shown by a thousand martyrs that we have no fear of the deeds of human beings. Desperation? Even in the most trying times Jewry has never been desperate but was always strengthened by its faith in God and by the consciousness of its right. Faith? Yes. Faith in the inner strength which is

The Jews lived a comfortable life in pre-Nazi Germany. This couple poses for a formal portrait on a winter vacation at the seashore.

born of the knowledge of events, and a clear conscience. Hope? Yes. The hope that coexistence through centuries with the German people will prove itself stronger than all prejudices.

Bruno Weil in Dawidowicz, *The War Against the Jews*, p. 234.

To truly understand how the German Jews (and the Jews of the rest of Europe) felt about the Nazis, Hitler, and the anti-Semitism of the Third Reich, you must try to see the world through their eyes. European Jews were lovers of logic, above all, of law and order. It was logic, law, and order—hallmarks of the European Enlightenment—that had opened the gates of the medieval ghettos, released the Jews, allowed them to educate themselves, and made them citizens of the countries of Europe. In the last two hundred years, they had made stupendous progress, becoming modern Jews—some fully assimilating or even converting. Most thought of themselves as patriotic citizens of Germany, France, Italy, and so forth. Even in the face of Nazism, the Jews of Europe believed that the world was still logical.

Jews line up in front of a Berlin travel agency selling tickets to Palestine immediately after *Kristallnacht*.

[They ask:] Why didn't you run away before? Before the borders were closed? Before the trap snapped shut?... [Most Jews] remained.... To emigrate one needed not only a lot of money but also a "bridgehead" in the country of destination: relatives or friends willing to offer sponsorship and/or hospitality.... The frontiers of Europe were practically closed, and England and the Americas had extremely reduced immigration quotas. Yet greater than this difficulty was another of an inner, psychological nature. This village or town or region or nation is mine, I was born here, my ancestors are buried here. I speak its language, have adopted its customs and culture; and to this culture I may even have contributed. I paid its [taxes], observed its laws. I fought its battles, not caring whether they were just or unjust. I risked my life for its borders, some of my friends or relations lie in the war cemeteries. ... I do not want to nor can I leave it; if I die I will die "in *patria* [the fatherland]"; that will be my way of dying "for the *patria*".

Primo Levi, *The Drowned and the Saved*, pp. 163-164.

Run Where?

Those who tried to run often found no way out. In 1924, the United States had passed the Johnson Immigration Act, which set a legal limit to the number of immigrants coming to the United States from any country. The names of German Jews applying to go to the United States were placed on a list. By 1939, the waiting period was four to five years. Countries such as France, Britain, Holland, and Belgium were all considered countries of transit—good places for the refugees to wait until the United States would accept them. All of these countries were filled with waiting refugees, and all took steps to close their borders in early 1939.

At the same time, the Nazis were eager to get Jews out of Germany. The Gestapo encouraged several shipping lines to sell visas to German Jews. The shipping agents charged anywhere from $150 to $300 per visa. Cuban visas were

German Jews view the harbor of Shanghai. Some refugees fled as far as Shanghai and others went on to Australia.

in high demand because Cuba was safely away from Europe, and very close to the United States.

This was the situation when the agents of the Hamburg-America Line sold visas to 907 Jews—734 of them already had numbers on the

May 13, 1939. Above, the Karliner family boards the ship *St. Louis*. Both parents and two of their four children were killed in the Holocaust. On June 2, 1939 *The New York Times* called the *St. Louis* "the saddest ship afloat" and placed its story on the front page.

U.S. quota waiting list. The Jews boarded the ship *St. Louis* bound for Cuba. In addition to exit visas, they had each paid about $150 for a "landing certificate" issued by the Cuban director-general of immigration. On May 5, 1939, the president of Cuba signed Decree No. 937, making all landing certificates invalid. Though the Hamburg-American Line knew, no one aboard the *St. Louis* was aware of this problem. On May 27, the ship entered the port of Havana, Cuba as the passengers on deck broke out in cheers and tears of gladness. Then came the bad news. The landing certificates were now "illegal." The 907 Jewish passengers could not land in Cuba.

CUBA ORDERS LINER AND REFUGEES TO GO

Navy to Escort St. Louis With 917 Aboard Unless She Obeys —Compromise Reported

By R. HART PHILLIPS

Wireless to THE NEW YORK TIMES.

HAVANA, June 1.—President Federico Laredo Bru today signed a decree ordering the Hamburg-American liner St. Louis to depart immediately with 917 Jewish refugees from Germany who have been held aboard the ship since Saturday awaiting permission to enter Cuba.

The decree provides, in case of non-compliance, that "the Secretary of the Treasury shall seek the aid of the constitutional navy and shall proceed to conduct the ship St. Louis, with passengers on board, outside the jurisdictional waters of Cuba." It is stipulated also that any member of the crew who may have debarked illegally shall be seized and conducted to the vessel.

The Treasury Department is directed to investigate the entire matter, including responsibility for bringing the refugees to Cuba.

To Leave at 10 A. M. Today

Captain Gustav Shroeder of the St. Louis tonight posted the following notice on the ship's bulletin boards:

"The Cuban Government requires us to leave the harbor but has allowed us to remain until tomorrow morning. So we shall sail definitely at 10 A. M.

> Anchored five days in the center of Havana harbor, [the ship] was now a tourist attraction. Friends and relatives of the refugees, lining the waterfront, were joined by Cuban sightseers. They produced a carnival atmosphere. Fruit and nut vendors set up shop on the Prado Promenade. . . . Binoculars and telescopes were rented. Entertainment was provided by street musicians and performing monkeys.
>
> Hysterical relatives tried to bribe policemen to get their families off the ship; the U.S. consulate was flooded with requests that America call a halt to all immigration from Germany so *St. Louis* passengers could enter without delay. . . .
>
> Thomas & Witts, *Voyage of the Damned*, pp. 192-193.

Some of the passengers gave up hope. There were even a few suicides and suicide attempts.

> [Max Loewe] slashed his wrists with a straight razor [and] leaped over the rail. . . . "Out! Out! Man overboard!". . . [Seaman Heinrich] Meier was one of the ship's best swimmers. Even so, the impact of the sea from the height he dived slapped hard against him. Underwater for seconds, he shot to the surface, and found his hands and body stained with Loewe's blood. Shouting filled his ears; Meier looked up, but could not make out the words. Then, from close by, he heard: "Murderers! They will never get me!". . . The seaman reached Max Loewe. . .grabbed him by the hair and pulled the desperate man to the surface. Loewe called out again: "Let me die!". . .[Meier] turned and saw the police boat; hands reached down and pulled Loewe out of the water. Moments later Meier too flopped into the launch. . . .
>
> Thomas & Witts, *Voyage of the Damned*, pp. 176-184.

A few minutes later the captain was informed that the passenger in cabin 76 on A–deck had locked the door from the inside and would not answer when called. The captain ordered that the door be forced open. Inside, they found a physician from Munich lying face up on his bed. On the bedstand was a syringe and a row of empty drug bottles. The purser asked the captain, "Will he live?" The captain said, "Who knows? And how many more will there be?"

For days, the *St. Louis* made front page headlines in all the world's major papers. After it left Havana, the ship sailed up and down the shoreline of Florida while the Joint Distribution Committee negotiated with the Cuban government. At one point, the JDC offered to post a $500 bond for every passenger on the ship, if the Cubans would allow them to enter. But in the end, the ship was forced to turn back to Europe, bound for Hamburg.

A short while earlier, the ship would have headed for Palestine, but the British had just limited to 10,000 the number of Jews that could enter Palestine each year. The JDC continued to try, even as the ship sailed. Finally, with the ship more than halfway back to Germany, France, Belgium, England, and the Netherlands each agreed to accept some of the passengers.

Not every boatload of refugees was as fortunate. In 1941, more than 750 Romanian Jews crowded aboard the small ship *Struma* bound for

Palestine. But the *Struma* was turned back by the British. The ship next sailed for Istanbul, Turkey. Burdened by its heavy load, the ship's engines gave out in the harbor. The Turks, however, refused to allow the Jews to land. Newspapers around the world devoted headlines to the *Struma*, but no nation offered a safe harbor. Seventy-four days after the journey began, the *Struma* sank in the Bosporus Sea, a few miles from the port of Istanbul. All but two of the passengers were drowned.

Why did the United States and other nations turn their back on the Jews of the *St. Louis*, the *Flandre*, the *Orduna*, the *Struma*, and other boatloads of refugees? There were many reasons: anti-Semitism, fear that some refugees might be Nazi agents, fear that refugees would take jobs from native workers by working for lower wages, fear that resources of the country would be stretched. One other reason is also worth mentioning. There were only half a million Jews in Germany, but there were millions more in Poland, Hungary, Austria, and other countries. If the borders were opened to the German Jews, wouldn't the other countries force their Jews to leave, too? Could any nation hope to receive so many refugees so suddenly without ruining itself?

A boatload of Jewish immigrants bound for Palestine. Leaving Europe by ship meant traveling in crowded and uncomfortable quarters, but it also meant a chance for safety and freedom.

REVIEW | ISSUES

■ As Germany annexed and conquered most of the countries of Europe, more and more Jews came under the Nazi heel. Yet the other nations of the world had shown that they wanted no more refugees. One Nazi writer boasted:

> We are saying openly that we do not want the Jews while the democracies keep on claiming that they are willing to receive them—and then leave them out in the cold. Aren't we savages better men after all?"
>
> *Der Weltkampf* in Lookstein, *Were We Our Brothers' Keepers?* p. 103.

■ Individual Jews of America and Great Britain tried time and again to help the Jews of Europe. One Jewish lawyer offered to raise a $50,000 bond if the U.S. government would only allow the *St. Louis* to anchor in New York harbor. But the doors of democracy were closed. The Jews of Europe had no way out.

■ This chapter speaks twice of suicide. Actually suicide was rare during the Holocaust. Judaism teaches that, since humans are created in God's image, taking one's own life is an insult to God. But in the years of the Crusades, the Jews were persecuted so fiercely that many took their own lives instead of falling into the hands of the Crusaders. This is called *kiddush hashem*, "the sanctification of God's name."

1. What is the difference between *kiddush hashem* and suicide?

2. Did the assimilated Jews of Germany commit *kiddush hashem* or suicide? Which did Max Loewe attempt?

■ At the height of the *St. Louis* crisis, a journalist in the *Jewish Daily Forward* wrote, "All Jews are on the *St. Louis* and we are all surrounded."

3. Explain what the journalist meant. Why did he feel this way?

■ Most Americans strongly favored the immigrant quota system in the 1930s and 1940s. A poll taken among Cincinnati women in May 1939 indicated that 77.3 percent opposed admitting "a considerable number of European refugee children outside the quota limits" while only 21.4 percent approved.

4. Should the United States throw open its borders today to accept refugees from Eastern Europe, Asia, Mexico, the Caribbean, Central and South America? Why? Why not?

IX
THE WAR AND THE JEWS

World conquest and the destruction of the Jews were linked in Hitler's mind. In March 1936, German troops marched into the Rhineland—a strip of land off-limits to Germans since the Treaty of Versailles. No government tried to stop him. In 1938, German troops occupied Austria. In 1939, Hitler took over Czechoslovakia. With each new conquest, the other nations watched, hoping Hitler would be satisfied. Hitler, however, continued to speak of *lebensraum*, "living space," for the Germans. Hitler was testing the waters—and no nation seemed ready to stop him.

The Nazi war against the Jews in these early years was also a testing of the waters. The Nazis tried to force Jews to leave Germany. But Jews who tried to leave found that there were few places to run—no nation seemed anxious to have them. Stories of the *St. Louis* and other boats made headlines in Germany just as they did in the rest of the world.

The War Begins

On September 1, 1939—with the *Luftwaffe* (the German air force) providing support—the German armies invaded Poland. Tanks and infantry moving quickly below, and planes above—this was the *Blitzkrieg* or "lightning war." The Polish army was no match for Germany. Against tanks and planes, the Poles fought on foot and horseback. Poland was defeated in five days.

On September 3, 1939, Britain and France finally declared war on Germany. World War II officially began. France and Britain (and later Russia) were the main Allied powers. The Allied armies were still weak; and, at home, the Allies still faced unemployment and lack of funds due to the Depression. The Axis powers were dictatorships—Germany, Italy, and Spain (later joined by Japan). Had the Allies attacked just after Hitler entered Poland, the war might have ended quickly. A great deal of

German war equipment had been damaged in Poland. Germany's troops were in Poland, far away from France.

For the moment, Russia was quiet—the Russian dictator Josef Stalin had agreed not to go to war with Hitler over Poland. Stalin had a better idea. When Hitler's troops were deep in Poland, Russia attacked Finland. Hitler was outraged. From Finland, Russia or the Allies could attack Norway and Denmark, coming at Germany from the north. Hitler knew he would have to wage war on two fronts—east and west—at the same time, but he did not count on fighting to the north as well. To end the northern threat, Hitler invaded Norway and Denmark, saying that he wanted to "protect" them.

Hitler next wanted to attack Russia to the east—to destroy his old enemy, the Communists. But he was afraid that France and Britain would choose that moment to attack him, forcing Germany to fight in both the east and the west. At last, he decided to turn westward. On May 10, 1940, Germany attacked Belgium and Holland. Both countries fell within days.

Polish cavalry was no match for the modern German air force, tanks, and infantry.

Hitler's Triumph

It was a clever plan. France and Britain were forced to march north to help Holland and Belgium, even as Hitler sent part of his army south toward France. In a matter of weeks, the Allied troops were trapped at Dunkirk with their backs to the sea. There were German armies to the north, south, and east of them, and four divisions of German tanks were closing in for the kill. Had Hitler pressed forward, he might have wiped out the combined forces of Britain and France at Dunkirk.

But Hitler made a mistake. He decided not to risk losing more men and equipment. He ordered the *Luftwaffe* to finish the job by bombing the Allied forces. In the greatest air battle of the war, the British Royal Air Force held off the *Luftwaffe* as more than 300,000 British, French, and Belgian soldiers were rescued from Dunkirk. Fishing boats, pleasure boats, even row boats were used to ferry Allied soldiers across the English Channel to safety. The Allied army was saved; but France was left unguarded. On June 21, 1940, France surrendered to Germany.

Allied soldiers escaping Dunkirk. Most of the Allied forces were rescued.

German paratroopers drop into Holland on the first day of the attack against Holland and Belgium.

The German people now hailed Hitler as the greatest military leader of modern times. He had defeated the French, Germany's most hated enemy, and sent the British running. He had conquered most of Europe. Hitler considered invading Britain. But between Europe and Britain was the sea; and Britain still had the strongest navy in the world. So Hitler planned to invade Russia instead.

Hitler's preparation to invade Russia was complete when his Italian allies attacked Greece. But Hitler's worst fears came true—Italy was far too weak to conquer Greece. Worried that the British would help Greece and then attack Germany from the south, Hitler was forced to send twenty-nine German divisions against Greece. The war in Greece was over in four weeks, but it was a month's delay that Hitler had not wanted.

The War in Russia

Hitler wanted help against Russia, but he had no luck. Italy was still too weak. Spain refused to keep the British busy in the west. Japan refused to attack Russia from the east. In the end, Hitler decided to act alone.

On June 22, 1941, three million German soldiers, over 7,000 cannons, and 3,500 tanks crossed the border into Russia. The Russian air force was quickly defeated. The aged Russian tanks were no match for Hitler's modern tanks. The Russian army lost battle after battle, constantly retreating toward Moscow. Russia was being defeated, but Hitler's *Blitzkrieg* had dragged to a crawl. Summer and fall passed; winter set in. It was October before the German army saw Moscow in the distance.

By December the temperature was below zero, and Moscow had not yet been taken. The German army was still wearing summer uniforms. The Russians had burned the crops behind them so that the Germans were forced to transport food from faraway Poland. German soldiers starved or died of exposure to the cold. Even Hitler realized that his armies had to be called back before they were utterly destroyed.

At the very moment that the German armies were suffering the worst, Japan attacked the United States. On December 7, 1941, the Japanese bombed Pearl Harbor in Hawaii. The United States immediately declared war on Japan and the Axis. Hitler's hours of victory were at an end. What followed were long, slow years of defeat.

When the Germans invaded Russia the second time, in the winter of 1942-43, they came prepared with warm uniforms.

The Other War

Behind the front lines, Hitler fought another war—a war against the Jews. As the German armies overran Europe, more and more Jews came under the Nazi heel. Everywhere, the Germans used propaganda to spread the lies of racism and anti-Semitism. They forced conquered countries to pass anti-Jewish laws like those in Germany.

What were Jews doing and thinking during these years of Hitler's triumph? One important piece of evidence was discovered in a pile of trash in a warehouse attic in Amsterdam, Holland. It is the diary of a young Dutch girl named Anne Frank. She was just thirteen years old when she began writing her diary. Her family had lived in Germany for centuries. She was very much like any American Jewish teenager today. "I have darling parents and a sister of sixteen," she wrote. "I know about 30 people whom one might call friends. . . . I have aunts and uncles, who are darlings, too, a good home, no—I don't seem to lack anything."

In 1933, when Anne was four years old, her family left Germany and settled in Amsterdam. Her father became managing director of a Dutch business. For seven years, things went well. But on May 10, 1940, the Nazis entered Holland, and four days later, hard times began.

> Jews must wear a yellow star, Jews must hand in their bicycles, Jews are banned from trains and are forbidden to drive, Jews are only allowed to do their shopping between three and five o'clock and then only in shops which bear the placard "Jewish

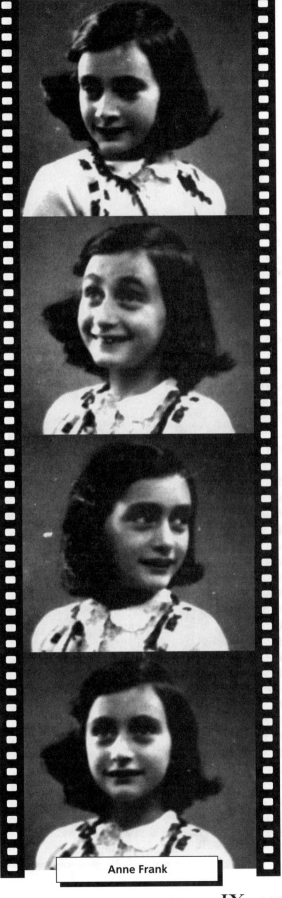

Anne Frank

shop." Jews must be indoors by eight o'clock and cannot even sit in their own gardens after that hour. Jews are forbidden to visit theaters, cinemas, and other places of entertainment. Jews may not take part in public sports. Swimming pools, tennis courts, hockey fields, and other sports grounds are all prohibited to them. Jews may not visit Christians. Jews must go to Jewish schools. . . . So we could not do this and were forbidden to do that.

Anne Frank, *The Diary of a Young Girl*, pp. 3-4.

The house in Amsterdam in which Anne Frank and her family hid.

Separation and Hiding

Two more years passed. Nazi laws separated Jews from their Dutch neighbors. Nazis rounded up many leading Jews and sent them to local concentration camps. Most non-Jews were afraid to help—the Gestapo punished those who helped Jews by sending them to the concentration camps, too. Only the bravest non-Jews raised a helping hand for families like the Franks.

The Franks prayed that the Allies would soon defeat Hitler and that they could remain hidden until the war was over. In July, 1942, the Frank family went through a door above a warehouse and seemingly vanished from the world. In their attic rooms which they called the "Secret Annex," Anne's diary—which she nicknamed "Kitty"—became her best friend.

> There are some large business premises on the right of us, and on the left a furniture workshop; there is no one there after working hours but even so, sounds could travel through the walls. We have forbidden Margot to cough at night, although she has a bad cold. . . . It is the silence that frightens me so in the evenings and at night. . . . I can't tell you how oppressive it is *never* to be able to go outdoors, also I'm very afraid that we shall be discovered and be shot. That is not exactly a pleasant prospect. We have to whisper and tread lightly during the day, otherwise the people in the warehouse might hear us.
>
> Anne Frank, *Diary of a Young Girl*, p. 19.

By October, 1942, the Germans were rounding up all of Holland's Jews. Anne was frightened.

> Dear Kitty,
>
> I've only got dismal and depressing news for you today. Our many Jewish friends are being taken away by the dozen. These people are treated by the Gestapo without a shred of decency, being loaded into cattle trucks and sent to Westerbork, the big Jewish camp in Drente. Westerbork sounds terrible. . . . There is no separate accommodations. Men, women, and children all sleep together. . . .
>
> It is impossible to escape; most of the people in the camp are branded as inmates by their shaven heads and many also by their Jewish appearance.
>
> If it is as bad as this in Holland, whatever will it be like in the distant and barbarous regions they are sent to? We assume that most of them are murdered. The English radio speaks of their being gassed.
>
> Anne Frank, *Diary of a Young Girl*, pp. 34-35.

No Jew was safe in Holland any longer.

> The Germans ring at every front door to inquire if there are any
> Jews living in the house. If there are then the whole family has to
> go at once. If they don't find any, they go on to the next house. No
> one has a chance of evading them unless one goes into hiding.
> Often they go around with lists, and only ring when they know
> they can get a good haul. . . . No one is spared—old people,
> babies, expectant mothers, the sick—each and all join in the
> march of death. . . .
>
> I feel wicked sleeping in a warm bed, while my dearest friends
> have been knocked down or have fallen into a gutter somewhere
> out in the cold night. I get frightened when I think of close friends
> who have now been delivered into the hands of the cruelest
> brutes that walk the earth. And all because they are Jews!.
>
> Anne Frank, *Diary of a Young Girl*, p. 48.

The Time of Hope

The Franks listened to the radio for news of the war. As Germany began
to lose the war, the Nazis became more fanatic in their program to murder the Jews. Instead of using trains to move German troops, the Nazis
continued to transport Jews to the death camps. In March of 1944, Hitler
invaded Hungary. Anne wrote, "Hungary is occupied by German troops.
There are still a million Jews there, so they too will have had it now."
Anne's thoughts were constantly turned to questions of life and death.
Her writing became more important to her.

> Anyone who doesn't write doesn't know how wonderful it is. . . . If I
> haven't any talent for writing books or newspaper articles, well,
> then I can always write for myself. . . .
>
> I want to go on living after my death! And therefore I am grateful
> to God for giving me this gift, this possibility of developing myself
> and of writing, of expressing all that is in me.
>
> Anne Frank, *Diary of a Young Girl*, p. 177.

The war had changed people, even the Dutch. Anne was disturbed
by the changes.

> To our great horror and regret we hear that the attitude of a great
> many people towards us Jews has changed. We hear that there is
> anti-Semitism now in circles that never thought of it before. This
> news has affected us all very, very deeply. The cause of this
> hatred of the Jews is understandable, even human sometimes, but
> not good. The Christians blame the Jews for giving secrets away
> to the Germans, for betraying their helpers and for the fact that,
> through the Jews a great many Christians have gone the way of so
> many others before them, and suffered terrible punishments and a
> dreadful fate.

Would Christians behave differently in our place? Why. . . should people demand the impossible of Jews?

We always hear that we're all fighting together for freedom, truth, and right! Is discord going to show itself while we are still fighting, is the Jew once again worth less than another? Oh, it is sad, very sad, that once more, for the umpteenth time, the old truth is confirmed: "What one Christian does is his own responsibility, what one Jew does is thrown back at all Jews."

Quite honestly, I can't understand that the Dutch, who are such a good, honest, upright people, should judge us like this, we, the most oppressed, the unhappiest, perhaps the most pitiful of all peoples of the whole world. . . .

And if [the Dutch fail us,] then the pitiful little collection of Jews that remain will have to leave Holland. We, too, shall have to move on again with our little bundles and leave this beautiful country, which offered us such a warm welcome and which now turns its backs on us.

Anne Frank, Diary of a Young Girl, pp. 214-215.

Suddenly there was hope. The Allied powers had invaded Europe. It was Tuesday, June 6, 1944.

English broadcast in German, Dutch, French, and other languages at ten o'clock: "The invasion has begun!" that means the "real" invasion. . . . "This is D-Day." General Eisenhower said to the French people: "Stiff fighting will come now, but after this the victory. The year 1944 is the year of complete victory; good luck."

Hope is revived within us; it gives us fresh courage, and makes us strong again. . . . Now more than ever we must clench our teeth and not cry out.

Oh, Kitty, the best part of the invasion is that I have the feeling that friends are approaching. We have been oppressed by those terrible Germans for so long, they have had their knives so at our throats, that the thoughts of friends and delivery fill us with confidence!

Anne Frank, Diary of a Young Girl, pp. 220-221.

The End of Hope

News of the fighting gave the people in the Secret Annex new confidence and strength. The war would soon be over. They might soon be rescued. Yet the war went on. In July, Anne wrote:

It's really a wonder that I haven't dropped all my ideals, because they seem so absurd and impossible to carry out. Yet I keep them, because in spite of everything I still believe that people are really good at heart. I simply can't build up my hopes on a foundation consisting of confusion, misery, and death. I see the world gradually being turned into a wilderness. I hear the ever approaching thunder, which will destroy us too. I can feel the sufferings of millions and yet, if I look up into the heavens, I think that it will all come right, that this cruelty too will end, and that peace and tranquility will return again. In the meantime, I must uphold my ideals, for perhaps the time will come when I shall be able to carry them out.

Anne Frank, Diary of a Young Girl, p. 237.

The last entry in Anne's diary is dated August 1, 1944. On August 4, the Secret Annex was discovered, and the Frank family was arrested. The Gestapo seized everything of value, leaving the papers, old books, magazines, and Anne's diary in a heap on the floor. In March 1945, before her sixteenth birthday, Anne died in the concentration camp at Bergen-Belsen. Otto Frank, Anne's father, was the only one of the family to survive the war. He was in the Auschwitz concentration camp when the Russian armies arrived. He returned to Holland, where his Dutch friends, who had protected Anne and her family for so long, gave him Anne's precious diary.

REVIEW | ISSUES

■ The Nazis under Hitler fought two wars—the military war (World War II), and the war against the Jews (the Holocaust). In both wars, they had their moments of triumph and victory. But in the end, they lost both wars.

■ It is clear how the Nazis lost the military war. They were outfought and out-thought. The Allied powers at first retreated in both the east and the west, only to regroup and return with greater strength.

■ In the next unit, it will become clear how the Nazis lost the other war, the war against the Jews. Though they managed to kill six million, they never managed to control the minds of the Jews. Spiritual strength, Jewish resistance, and hope—qualities exemplified in the diary of Anne Frank—were the only weapons the Jews had. Yet, despite the Nazi's greatest efforts, the Jewish people and Judaism survived the war.

■ Some historians have speculated that the Nazis' plans for the Jews affected the rest of the Nazi war effort.

1. How did World War II affect the Nazi plan for the Jews?
2. How did the military war make the assault on the Jews easier for the Nazis?
3. Why did the Nazis use trains for transporting Jews even when the trains were needed for their war effort?

■ As the anti-Jewish laws separated Jews from their neighbors, some neighbors tried to help. Others gave only sympathetic looks.

4. What is the difference between being sympathetic to the suffering of others and actively helping?
5. Why did most people not help? Why did some non-Jews help?

■ Anne said she felt guilty because she was safe while other Jews were suffering. Many Jews who survived the Holocaust continued to feel guilty about being alive when their friends and family had died.

6. Is this guilty feeling logical? Can you explain it?

■ Anne Frank noted that "What one Christian does is his own responsibility, what one Jew does is thrown back at all Jews."

7. Can you explain what this means? Is it true today?
8. Have you ever felt this way?

UNIT THREE

RESISTANCE, RESCUE, AND JUSTICE

X
RESISTANCE
PAGE 116

XI
WHEN DID THE WORLD LEARN OF THE HOLOCAUST?
PAGE 130

XII
THE RIGHTEOUS FEW
PAGE 140

XIII
A STRUGGLE TO THE DEATH
PAGE 152

XIV
WAR CRIMES AND PUNISHMENT
PAGE 164

X
RESISTANCE

After the war, historians gave the name "Holocaust" to the Nazi Final Solution. The dictionary defines *holocaust* as a raging fire consuming in its path all that lives. In translating the Bible, *holocaust* has another meaning. It is a sacred sacrifice—a burnt offering. The Hebrew word used for the Holocaust is *shoah* (pronounced "show-ah"), meaning a sudden collapse or devastation. These words will always carry special meaning for us.

Because the world of the Holocaust was a living hell, most survivors wanted to forget it as quickly as possible. But the world wanted to know, why didn't the Jews fight back? Why did so many Jews go to their deaths without a struggle?

Slowly, the survivors began to tell their stories. More and more of the truth came out. In fact, the story continues to grow, as historians continue to probe the past. The Jews did fight back—not in just one place but in most places, and not in just one way but in many ways.

Evidence

Evidence of Jewish resistance comes mainly from testimony of survivors and documents. Photographs of Jews revolting against Nazi rule are extremely rare. There is a simple explanation for this. Most Holocaust photos were taken by the Germans. They were snapshots meant to glorify the soldiers or the SS men. The Nazi photographers did not want proof of Jewish revolts and uprisings. Also, during revolts and uprisings, there was no time for Nazis to take snapshots.

Many photos were part of official records of the Gestapo, the army, or the *Einsatzgruppen*. Others were merely mementos, the kind of photographs we take on vacation. Almost all of the photographs were seized by Allied troops during raids on Nazi offices, or taken from captured German soldiers. So there is little photographic evidence of Jewish resistance.

But there was much resistance, in the ghettos, in the forests, in the death camps. And, too, there was a quiet, heroic resistance in the hearts of the Jews, a spiritual resistance. This chapter tells only a few stories of Jewish resistance. For every one story told here, there are ten or twenty, a hundred or a thousand more that could be told.

Spiritual Resistance

In the ghettos and the concentration camps, Jews continued to hope. In the ghettos they still had a few reasons to hope—families, neighborhoods, community. In the concentration camps, everything was taken away from them. They were left

> to toil the whole day in the wind, with the temperature below freezing, and wearing only a shirt, underpants, cloth jacket, and trousers, and in one's body nothing but weakness, hunger, and knowledge of the end drawing near.
>
> Primo Levi, *If This Is a Man*, pp. 112-113.

In this photograph, Jews are being marched along a side road. In a few moments, they will be executed by the German soldiers.

How can we understand what it means to lose everything? In the language of the camps, a *musselman* was a person whose eyes were dead, a walking corpse. Everyone knew that the *musselman* would soon die—of disease, of starvation, or by being selected to be sent to the death camps by the Nazis. Yet many Jews never became so totally empty in their souls. Many survived. Why?

One key to survival was pure chance—some Jews were just lucky. Another key was the will to survive. After the first few days in the camps, some Jews promised themselves that they would survive. They did whatever they could to make their promise come true. A third key was staying as clean as possible. Those who continued to wash—even in dirty water and without soap—stood a better chance against disease. A fourth key was the wish to bear witness—to tell the world about the horrors of the camp. Some Jews looked to the future, hoping that, if humanity learned how horrible the camps were, nothing like this would ever happen again. A fifth key was family. Some Jews swore that they would survive so that at least one of their family would live on. Except for pure chance, all of these keys to survival were forms of inner or "spiritual" resistance.

> Religious Jews, Zionists, and Communists often seemed to survive better than assimilated Jews. The individual who possessed a religious or political ideology often resisted Nazi horror. . . .
>
> Robbin, "Life in the Camps," in Grobman & Landes, *Genocide*, p. 239.

When surviving was impossible, many Jews met death nobly. Religious Jews called this a sacrifice *al kiddush hashem*, "to glorify God." They firmly believed that God would come to the aid of the Jewish people, that the Germans would be defeated and punished for what they had done. Facing the firing squads, one rabbi told his people:

> We are suffering the worst fate of all Jewish generations. In a few minutes we will fall into this open grave, and nobody will even know where we are buried nor recite a prayer for us. And we yearn so much to live. . . . In this moment let us unite. . . . Let us face the Germans with joy for glorifying the Lord's name.
>
> Rabbi Nachum of Kowel in Hausner, *Justice in Jerusalem*, p. 185

In the roundups, on the trains, in the forests waiting to be shot, rabbis and community leaders spoke to their people of hope. In the dark days of the Vilna ghetto, a poet, Hirsh Glik, set these words to the melody of a Russian composer:

> Never say this is the final road for you,
> Though darkening skies may hide the days of blue.
> The hour that we longed for is so near,
> Our step beats out the message—we are here!
>
> From lands green with palms to lands all white with snow,
> We shall be coming with our anguish and our woe,
> And where a drop of our blood fell on the earth,
> There our courage and our spirit have rebirth.

The early morning sun makes bright our day,
And yesterdays with our foe will fade away.
But if the sun delays and in the east remains—
This song as slogan, generations must maintain.

This song written with our blood; not with lead,
It's not a little tune that birds sing overhead,
This song a people sang amid collapsing walls,
With grenades in hand they heeded to the call.

So never say the road now ends for you,
Though darkening skies may hide the days of blue.
The hour that we longed for is so near—
Our step beats out the message—we are here!.

Hirsh Glik in Mlotek & Gottlieb, We Are Here, p. 94.

Some attempted escape—from ghettos or camps. Jews who escaped the camps brought news of the mass killings back to the ghettos. One Jew who escaped even managed to smuggle a photograph of the ovens to London. But few escapes were successful. And many Jews refused to try escape because they knew that the Nazis would put to death an entire barracks or a group of Jews if any one of them escaped.

There were other kinds of spiritual resistance: Jews in the ghetto forged passports and papers for one another. They secretly listened to Allied radio broadcasts and reprinted the news they heard in underground newspapers. Even in the camps, Jews continued to study Judaism with rabbis and teachers. They celebrated Jewish holidays, using bits of fat they might have eaten to light as Sabbath "candles." Though they were being put to death because they were Jews, they resisted to the end by remaining Jewish.

Ghetto Revolts

Jews in Nieswiez managed to smuggle a machine gun into the ghetto piece by piece. When the Germans came to select some Jews for deportation on July 21, 1942,

> The members of the underground and the mass of Jews standing at the gate replied resolutely, "No! There will be no selection! If some are to live, then all must; if not, we shall defend ourselves!" ... The Germans opened fire. The fighting unit in the synagogue answered with a surprise volley of machine-gun fire. The Germans crashed through the ghetto gate. The Jews drew their knives and iron [bars]. They reached for their piles of stones. ... A battle began between Jews with steel weapons and Germans and police with guns. ... Soon the ghetto was filled with dead and dying. Throughout the streets, bodies lay like discarded puppets. ... Small groups of Jews like ours burst forth from the ghetto. Once outside, some were beaten by zealous peasants. Others were killed in flight. Small groups succeeded in reaching the forest.

Shalom Cholawski in Gilbert, The Holocaust, pp. 383-384.

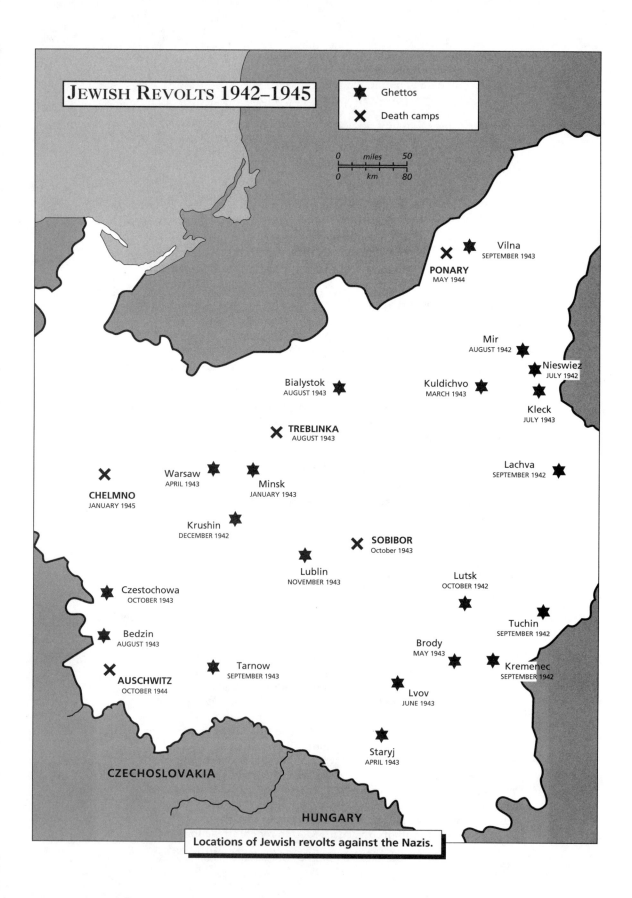

JEWISH REVOLTS 1942–1945

★ Ghettos

✗ Death camps

0 ⊢miles⊣ 50
0 ⊢km⊣ 80

✗ ★ Vilna
PONARY SEPTEMBER 1943
MAY 1944

Mir ★
AUGUST 1942
★ Nieswiez
JULY 1942

Bialystok ★   Kuldichvo ★
AUGUST 1943   MARCH 1943   ★ Kleck
JULY 1943

✗ TREBLINKA
AUGUST 1943

✗   Warsaw ★ ★ Minsk   Lachva ★
CHELMNO   APRIL 1943 JANUARY 1943   SEPTEMBER 1942
JANUARY 1945

Krushin ★
DECEMBER 1942

★ Lublin   ✗ SOBIBOR
NOVEMBER 1943   October 1943

Lutsk ★
OCTOBER 1942

★ Czestochowa
OCTOBER 1943   Tuchin ★
SEPTEMBER 1942

★ Bedzin   Brody ★
AUGUST 1943   MAY 1943   ★ Kremenec
SEPTEMBER 1942

★ Tarnow
✗ AUSCHWITZ   SEPTEMBER 1943   ★ Lvov
OCTOBER 1944   JUNE 1943

★ Staryj
APRIL 1943

CZECHOSLOVAKIA

HUNGARY

Locations of Jewish revolts against the Nazis.

German soldiers firing into ghetto buildings. In the background, other buildings are already ablaze.

Most of the rebels were hunted down and killed. A few escaped to join partisan groups in the forests to fight against the Nazis. In some revolts, no Jews survived to tell the tale.

In most ghettos, it was young people—mainly Socialists, Communists, and Zionists—who organized the revolts. These young people were all members of radical groups—even before the war they had wanted to change Jewish society. Trapped by the Nazis, they organized fighting units, urging other Jews to join them. The young leaders were the first to believe rumors about concentration camps and mass murder. They smuggled guns into the ghettos and trained themselves to use them. Often, teenage girls and young women acted as messengers, slipping out of one ghetto into another, carrying news and smuggling weapons, always risking their lives.

Armed revolts broke out in ghettos like Krakow, Warsaw, Vilna, and Bialystok. At Krakow, the Jews organized a surprise attack outside the ghetto. On December 22, 1942, the Jewish Fighting Organization raided a coffee house where Gestapo and SS men gathered. Adolf Liebeskind, a leader of the revolt, was killed in the fighting. A few weeks before, he said, "We are fighting for three lines in the history books." After the revolt, a few Jews managed to escape to the forest.

Another revolt was organized by Jews in a labor camp in Volhynia. They collected a small pile of knives, iron bars, bricks, and a single pistol and placed them all in the carpentry shop. The Nazis came on Shabbat, December 12, 1942. One carpenter opened fire with the pistol, others scattered acid to burn the Germans. The Germans withdrew from the camp and fired on the Jews from afar. Later that day, the Germans returned and the battle continued. By evening the revolt was over. Those Jews who had not died in the fighting were put to death afterward.

The Warsaw Ghetto Uprising

The most famous ghetto revolt took place in Warsaw. It was led by the Zionists. They planned it far in advance. Guns and ammunition were smuggled into the ghetto. Bottles filled with gasoline and sealed with rags became homemade anti-tank bombs that could be set aflame and thrown. As the Jews prepared, however, the Nazis continued rounding up Jews in Warsaw to send to the concentration camps.

In January 1943, with only 70,000 Jews left in the ghetto, a small revolt broke out. Heinrich Himmler himself came to see what was happening. Based on his visit, he decided that it was time to transport all the Jews to death camps and destroy the Warsaw ghetto.

> The night of April 18 [1943] the final act of the tragedy of the Warsaw ghetto began. It was intended as a birthday gift for the Fuhrer. . . . At 6:00 a.m. [on April 19] a contingent of 2,000 heavily-armed SS men entered the Central Ghetto, with tanks, machine guns, three trailers loaded with ammunition, and ambulances. . . . The Jewish population was nowhere to be seen; all were hidden in underground bunkers or other hiding places. Only [the resistance organization] was on the alert above ground.
>
> Yitzhak Zuckerman in Dawidowicz, *A Holocaust Reader*, p. 375.

When the German tanks rolled into the ghetto, 1,000 Jewish fighters were ready for them. The Jews had 3 machine guns, about 80 rifles, hand grenades, gasoline bombs, and perhaps 300 pistols and revolvers. The Germans were taken by surprise. Grenades and bombs blew up the leading German tanks, blocking the entrance to the ghetto and forcing the Germans to retreat.

April 19 was also the first evening of Passover. One of the fighters was searching for flashlights in a ghetto building. She suddenly came upon a family celebrating a *Seder*.

> Wandering about there, I unexpectedly came upon Rabbi Maisel. . . . The room looked as if it had been hit by a hurricane. Bedding was everywhere, chairs lay overturned, the floor was strewn with household objects, the window panes were all gone.
>
> Amidst this destruction, the table in the center of the room looked [out of place] with glasses filled with wine, with the family seated around, the rabbi reading the *Haggadah*. His reading was punctuated by explosions and the rattling of machine guns; the faces of the family around the table were lit by the red light from the burning buildings nearby. . . . I could not stay long. As I was leaving, the rabbi cordially bade me farewell and wished me success. He was old and broken, he told me, but we, the young people, must not give up, and God would help us.
>
> Tuvia Borzykowski in Gilbert, *The Holocaust*, p. 559.

The next day, in revenge, the Germans broke into a Jewish hospital. "German soldiers went through the wards shooting and killing all whom

German troops set fire to buildings in the Warsaw ghetto to kill the Jews in hiding.

they found. Then they set the building on fire. Those patients and staff who had managed to reach the cellars died in the fire."

> [On] the second day of the action. . . a group of 300 SS men approached the gate of the brushworks area. They stopped [long enough for] our fighters to explode an electrically-operated mine under the SS men's feet. The Germans fled, leaving 80-100 dead and wounded. Two hours later they returned. . . . Thirty Germans entered, but only two got out. . . . Only then did the Germans call in their artillery. . . . This was the second total victory for the fighters. . . . The Germans started setting fire to the ghetto on the second day of the action. . . . In response. . . the fighters set fire to all the [warehouses and] shop stores, worth several tens of millions of zlotys.
>
> Yitzhak Zuckerman in Dawidowicz, *A Holocaust Reader*, p. 376.

Days of fighting followed. The Germans tried searching one building at a time for the hidden Jews, but wherever they turned, they found resistance fighters. One after another, German soldiers fell. The fighting was so intense that the German commander sent for more troops. A week passed, then two. The Jews were running out of ammunition. They used weapons taken from dead German soldiers. The Germans used flame throwers, artillery, and even called in aircraft to drop bombs. Building after building was reduced to rubble.

The battle continued until May 8 when the Germans finally reached the central command post of the Jewish fighters. Over a hundred fighters fell in that one building. In the end, the Germans threw gas bombs into the bunker to kill the last leaders of the resistance. Inside the fighters discussed what to do.

> Aryeh Wilner was the first to cry out: "Come, let us destroy ourselves. Let's not fall into their hands alive." The suicides began. Pistols jammed and the owners begged their friends to kill them. But no one dared to take the life of a comrade. . . . Then someone discovered a hidden exit, but only a few succeeded in getting out this way. The others slowly suffocated in the gas.
>
> Zivia Lubetkin in Gilbert, *The Holocaust*, pp. 564-565.

Jews captured during the revolt are marched out of the Warsaw ghetto.

Warsaw Jews being forced out of an underground bunker in which they had been hiding.

On May 16 the German commander reported to Himmler that the Warsaw ghetto "is no longer in existence." Then the Germans blew up the Warsaw synagogue, though no one seemed to be in it. One by one, they destroyed the buildings. Small groups of Jews continued to live in hollowed-out bunkers below these buildings. The last group was not discovered until September. Some Jews escaped through the sewers during the fighting. Others made their way into "Aryan" Warsaw and then to the forests. But the destruction in Warsaw was nearly total.

News of the Warsaw ghetto revolt spread through the concentration and labor camps, inspiring many more revolts. The Jews of Warsaw had proved—to themselves and to the whole world—that they could fight as fiercely as any people on earth.

Partisans

Those who escaped from trains, from ghettos, even from concentration camps fled to the forests. There they joined underground movements—partisan fighters. Some Polish partisan groups permitted Jews to join. Other groups were anti-Semitic, hating Jews almost as much as the Nazis did. Sometimes the Jews just formed their own partisan bands. One freedom fighter remembered:

> Our first days in the forest were very difficult. It rained without letup and we had neither shelter nor food.
>
> After many days. . . two girls from our group came accidentally upon a patrol of Russian partisans. The happiness at our discovering each other was mutual. . . .

The Russian partisans remained with us for some time and thanks to them we were better armed. We carried out joint operations. . . .

From time to time the Germans, with the aid of the Ukranian police, raided the forest. . . . In the winter of 1943 when it already became apparent to the Ukranians that Hitler was losing the war they did everything possible to exterminate the armed Jewish groups [because the partisans] were the living witnesses of what had happened and they would tell the [Allies] how eagerly the Ukranians collaborated with the Germans in the annihilation of the Jews.

Joshua Wermuth in Suhl, *They Fought Back*, pp. 227-228.

The bands of Jewish freedom fighters were made up mainly of teenagers—young men and women. They stole or bought guns, attacking the Germans whenever and wherever possible. They came out of hiding to strike at the Nazis, then faded back into the cover of the forest where the army could not easily follow them. A few of these groups managed to survive to the end of the war.

Resistance in the Camps

Jews in the ghetto had some contact with the outside world. They could smuggle in guns and ammunition. In the concentration and death camps, the situation was far different. The Jews were entirely cut off. Revolts were much more difficult. Nevertheless, the Jews did revolt. In August 1943, when survivors from the Warsaw ghetto were sent by train to the death camp at Treblinka, they carried both news of the uprising and a few concealed weapons. The Jewish workers of Treblinka decided that this was the moment for the revolt they had been planning.

We were able to get one of our comrades into the [ammunition] building. . . . [We] cut a pane out of a window opposite the door. . . . A cart driven by a member of our group drove up to the building [pretending to remove garbage]. Under it twenty hand grenades, twenty rifles, and several revolvers with cartridges were loaded [to be] divided among the combat units.

We had gotten some gasoline from trucks and tanks in the garage through one of our comrades, a mechanic. . . . On the day of the [revolt] the gasoline. . . was sprinkled. . . .

At 3:45 p.m. we heard the signal—a rifle shot near the gates of the Jewish barracks. This was followed by the detonations of hand grenades hurled at [the gasoline]. An enormous fire broke out in the whole camp. The arsenal exploded and everything was burned. . . .

The victim of the first shot was. . . the chief of the guards. . . . Of the 700 [Jewish] workers on the camp grounds, only 150 to 200 suc-

French Jewish partisans celebrate the end of the war.

ceeded in escaping, the others perished in the camp as well as
more than 20 Germans. Of the 150 to 200 who managed to escape,
only 12 are still alive; the others were later murdered by the German hangmen.

Samuel Rajzman in Suhl, *They Fought Back*, pp. 131-132.

Throughout the Jewish resistance, women fought as bravely as men.
At Auschwitz, a Jewish woman named Mala Zimetbaum became a symbol
of courage and defiance. She stole an SS uniform and German documents
telling of the slaughter at the death camp. She escaped, only to be recap-
tured and sent back to Auschwitz. The Nazis paraded her in front of the
whole camp. Suddenly, she began to slash her own wrist with a razor.
She was stopped by an SS officer, but Mala slapped him across the face.
"Don't be afraid, girls," she yelled, "their end is near. I am certain of this.
I know. I was free." The Nazis beat her, then burned her alive. In 1944, a
revolt broke out in Birkenau. Using smuggled sticks of dynamite, the
Jewish women blew up one of the furnaces. As always, the cost of the
revolt was high. All of the women were captured, tortured, and finally
hanged.

Most resistance ended in death. These two young Jewish partisans were captured, put on display, and then hanged by Germans.

■ Almost all the Jews who chose to fight were doomed. Yet those who fought felt their deaths would mean more if they died in battle. Escape was seldom a good choice. Except for the forest, there was no place to run. Even counting the forest, there was really no safe place to hide. Jewish physical resistance came in the face of almost certain death. No one believed that resisting would seriously hurt the Nazis. In all of the revolts and all of the partisan actions, only a few thousand Germans were killed.

■ Spiritual resistance showed bravery and defiance, but it, too, usually ended in death. German documents captured after the war tell how Jews went into the gas chambers praying and singing. Even in the crowded gas chambers, individuals spoke bravely to the group. Always they repeated their faith: that the Germans would soon be defeated and Judaism would survive. The spiritual resistance, however, had another effect: Nazi officers were amazed by it. They could not understand how people they thought "inferior" could die with such dignity. Through resistance—military and spiritual—the worst moment in Jewish history actually became one of the greatest moments of Jewish pride.

■ The right to self-defense has a long tradition in Judaism. Although Judaism deplores killing, it is permitted to kill when one's life is in danger and no alternative can be found. In Exodus [22:1-2] we read, "If the thief is caught while tunneling, and he is beaten to death, there is no sin in that case." The rabbis said this meant that people are innocent when they are forced to kill in self-defense.

1. Did Jews have a choice during the years of the Holocaust?

2. How do you think Jewish law would rule about the guilt or innocence of partisans?

■ Several times the chapter stresses the fact that most of the leaders of the resistance, and the partisans in the forests, were teenagers and young men and women.

3. Why would young people be more likely to resist than their elders?

4. Why were Zionists, Communists, and Socialists the most likely to resist? Define Zionism, Communism, and Socialism.

5. How do stories of the Jewish resistance during the Holocaust make you feel? Which resistance was more powerful in your opinion, the military resistance or the spiritual resistance? Why?

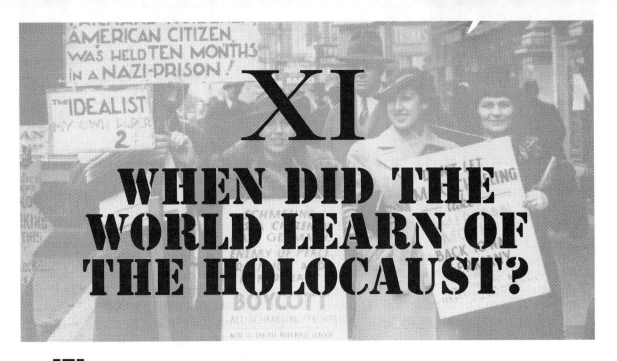

XI
WHEN DID THE WORLD LEARN OF THE HOLOCAUST?

The question of precisely when people in the free world first learned of the Holocaust is difficult to answer. On April 15, 1945, British troops reached the concentration camp at Bergen-Belsen. A war correspondent, reporting on the camp that day, began by saying, "It is my duty to describe something beyond the imagination of mankind." Was this really the first time that he had imagined what was happening to the Jews in Nazi Europe?

Corpses of murdered Jews found by the British army when they liberated the camp at Bergen-Belsen, in April 1945.

Early Reports

The *Einsatzgruppen* (see Chapter 4) began the work of mass killings in the summer of 1941. In November 1941, newspapers in New York and London reported that 52,000 Jews had been murdered by Nazis in Kiev. In March 1942, a short article in a London paper reported that all the Jews in Mariupol had been slaughtered. In April 1942, a London *Sunday Times* reporter stationed in Turkey learned that 120,000 Romanian Jews had been killed. His story also became a minor news item.

Newspapers in places like New York, London, Sweden, and Switzerland all carried stories of mass murders of Jews. Always these were minor stories, seldom front-page news. Newspapers saved the front pages for news of the fighting war. The London *Daily Telegraph* was the first to speak of an organized anti-Jewish program. On June 25, 1942, an article in the *Daily Telegraph* began "More than 700,000 Polish Jews have been slaughtered by the Germans in the greatest massacres in the world's history."

The report spoke of mass killings in Russia, the use of gas vans, and the camp at Chelmno. Five days later, the same newspaper carried the headline, "MORE THAN 1,000,000 JEWS KILLED IN EUROPE." This time the *Daily Telegraph* said it was the Nazi aim

> to wipe the [Jewish] race from the European continent. . . . It is estimated that the casualties suffered by the Jewish people in Axis-controlled countries already far exceed those of any other race in any war. . . .
>
> Cited in Laqueur, "Hitler's Holocaust," *Encounter*, Vol. LV, 1, p. 11.

Not everyone agreed. For example, Hebrew newspapers in Palestine complained about "unproven and exaggerated rumors" of Jewish deaths and even accused English-language papers of trying to outdo one another in reporting gruesome stories. Marie Syrkin, a leading Jewish journalist, remembers discussing early reports of the Holocaust with her editor at the *Jewish Frontier*, Hayim Greenberg. They agreed that the reports were "the macabre fantasy of a lunatic sadist." They printed a note in small type in the back of the September 1942 issue of the *Jewish Frontier* saying that some people believed there was a plan to exterminate the Jews of Europe. It can still be seen there today, Ms. Syrkin later said, as "a monument to our gross stupidity." Despite the many brief media accounts of mass killings, even Hebrew newspapers and Jewish reporters could not believe that the Germans were ready to kill all the Jews of Europe.

How Did the Truth Come Out?

In May 1942 the Socialist *Bund* headquarters in the Warsaw ghetto smuggled a report to London saying that 700,000 European Jews had been killed so far. The report was given to Shmuel Zygelbojm, who had been a member of the *Bund* underground in Warsaw. Zygelbojm had escaped Warsaw in December 1939. Zygelbojm gave a copy of the report to Gerhard Riegner, the World Jewish Congress representative in Switzerland. Zygelbojm also told the story on radio; and he was the one who gave the story to the *Daily Telegraph*.

In a June press conference, the World Jewish Congress announced that more than one million Jews had been murdered already. Eastern Europe was being turned into "a vast slaughterhouse for Jews," they said. Newspapers throughout the free world carried headlines regarding the mass murders. In the United States, the American Jewish Congress, B'nai B'rith, the Jewish Labor Committee, and other organizations held a mass rally in Madison Square Garden. Twenty thousand people listened to Jewish speakers and heard a message from President Roosevelt

American Jewish concern for the fate of Europe's Jews began in 1933. In March 1938, Jews in New York organized picket lines to boycott stores selling Nazi goods.

promising that guilty Nazis would be punished as soon as the war was won. A million Jews had been killed, but most people still did not believe that the Nazis meant to wipe out all the Jews of Europe.

On August 1, 1942, Riegner got proof. He met with a German who was visiting Switzerland "on business." The German, an anti-Nazi, told Riegner that Hitler had ordered the extermination of all of the Jews of Europe in one Final Solution. Riegner still could hardly believe his ears. He knew that the Jews of Belgium, Holland, and France were being sent to Poland, and that the Jews of the Warsaw ghetto were being "resettled" somewhere else. But now there was little reason to doubt—a holocaust was happening. Riegner sent the following telegram to Rabbi Stephen S. Wise in New York and to Sydney Silverman (a Member of Parliament) in London:

> Received alarming report that in Fuhrer's headquarters plan discussed and under consideration according to which all Jews in countries occupied or controlled [by] Germany numbering 3 1/2-4 millions should after deportation and concentration in east be exterminated at one blow to resolve once and for all Jewish question in Europe STOP The action reported planned for autumn methods under discussion including prussic acid STOP We transmit information with all reservation as exactitude cannot be confirmed STOP Informant stated to have close connections with the highest German authorities generally speaking reliable.
>
> Gerhard Riegner in Lookstein,
> *Were We Our Brothers' Keepers?* p. 108.

Rabbi Stephen S. Wise, a founder and president of the American Jewish Congress.

Acting on the News

Rabbi Wise took his copy of the Riegner telegram to the U.S. Undersecretary of State. The State Department asked for time to check the telegram's truth. Would Rabbi Wise agree not to announce the news until they were positive that it was true? Wise agreed. For three months he waited, wondering why it was taking so long, and wondering if he had made a mistake in agreeing to wait. It was November before the State Department admitted that the telegram was accurate. They gave Wise permission to inform the press. In a press conference held on November 24, 1942, Wise told reporters that nearly half of Europe's Jews had been murdered.

The Jewish world was jolted by this announcement. For seven days, Hebrew newspapers in Palestine bordered their front pages in black as a sign of mourning. On December 2, Jews in thirty countries held a day of prayer and fasting.

On December 8, Wise and other American Jewish leaders met with President Franklin D. Roosevelt directly. The President expressed sympathy for the losses of the Jewish people, adding, "We are doing everything possible to [determine] who [among the Nazis] are personally guilty."

The rest of the free world reacted to the news, too. On December 17, 1942, eleven governments of the free world issued a joint statement saying:

> The German authorities. . . are now carrying into effect Hitler's oft-repeated intention to exterminate the Jewish people in Europe. From all the occupied countries Jews are being transported in conditions of appalling horror and brutality to Eastern Europe. . . . None of those taken away are ever heard of again. The able-bodied are slowly worked to death in labor camps. The infirm are left to die of exposure and starvation or are deliberately massacred in mass executions. The number of victims of these bloody cruelties is reckoned in many hundreds of thousands of entirely innocent men, women, and children.
>
> The [eleven] governments. . . condemn in the strongest possible terms this bestial policy of cold-blooded extermination. . . . Those responsible for these crimes shall not escape retribution. . . .
>
> *The New York Times*, December 18, 1942.

This statement was read aloud in the U.S. Congress, in Parliament in London, and in many other countries as well. In London, members of Parliament stood for two full minutes of silence—an act which, in the whole long tradition of the British Parliament, had always been reserved only for the death of a monarch. Headlines about the Holocaust appeared this time on the front pages of newspapers throughout the free world.

What Could Be Done?

The editor of the American Hebrew weekly *Hadoar* wrote "The news was enough to drive one insane."

Solomons—Warship Hit

By CHARLES HURD.
Special to The New York Times.

WASHINGTON, Dec. 17 — A group of Army Flying Fortresses operating in the Solomon Islands on Wednesday destroyed an entire force of twelve Japanese Zero fighter planes that attacked the Americans in the vicinity of New Georgia Island, the Navy reported in a communiqué issued here to-day. One of the Flying Fortresses was lost but its crew was rescued.

This is one of the most notable air victories yet achieved by our bombers in combat with enemy fighter planes, although Army Air Force records have shown consistently for a long period an advantage of about six to one enjoyed by American heavy bombers in contests with both the Japanese Zeros and up-to-date German fighting planes, such as the Messerschmitt 109-G and Focke-Wulf 190.

It was considered probable here

Continued on Page Twelve

ws Summarized

AY, DECEMBER 18, 1942

Secretary of State Hull told his press conference that all elements "should strive to unify their efforts" to help the Allied military cause until final success. "We need all the help we can get," he said. [5:1.]

Moscow announced that stubborn German defenses had been overpowered southwest of Stalingrad on the railway leading to Kotelnikov, ninety miles away, after a fierce battle lasting two

---

alarm until the all-clear was sounded. In the Times Square area and elsewhere there was a considerable amount of confusion as lights went on, pedestrians started to move and traffic began to roll at the second audible signal.

This signal was evidently mistaken for the all-clear by many of the thousands of amusement seekers on the streets at the time. It appeared that some at least of the more than 50,000 air raid wardens who had responded to the preliminary yellow signal were also confused, for some of them gave conflicting instructions to the bewildered men and women who were trying to obey instructions.

The yellow signal, mobilizing the city's protective services and relayed to such important centers of activity as railroads, utilities, war factories, hospitals and theatres, went out at 8:56 P. M. The first audible signal was sounded on the sirens at 9:20, when the blue signal, which has hitherto been confidential, was flashed from Police Headquarters.

At that time many of the stores in the Broadway amusement area began to black out and scores of pedestrians began to seek shelter in doorways and theatre lobbies. Apparently there were a great many people who had failed to grasp the instructions made public by Mayor La Guardia to regard the first audible signal merely as a warning.

Broadway was almost completely darkened within a minute after the sounding of the first audible alarm and there was little activity on the streets. Policemen and air raid wardens, however, began passing the word as generally as they could

Continued on Page Eighteen

---

11 ALLIES CONDEMN NAZI WAR ON JEWS

United Nations Issues Joint Declaration of Protest on "Cold-Blooded Extermination"

Special to The New York Times.

WASHINGTON, Dec. 17 — A joint declaration by members of the United Nations was issued to-day condemning Germany's "bestial policy of cold-blooded extermination" of Jews and declaring that "such events can only strengthen the resolve of all freedom-loving peoples to overthrow the barbarous Hitlerite tyranny."

The nations reaffirmed "their solemn resolution to insure that those responsible for these crimes shall not escape retribution and to press on with the necessary practical measures to this end."

The declaration was issued simultaneously through the State Department here and in London. It was subscribed to by eleven nations, including the United States, Britain and Russia, and also by the French National Committee in London.

The declaration referred particularly to the program as conducted in Poland and to the barbarous forms it is taking.

TEXT OF DECLARATION

The attention of the Belgian, Czechoslovak, Greek, Luxem-

Continued on Page Ten

> Here is how the joint statement of the eleven allied nations appeared on the front page of *The New York Times*, December 18, 1942.

And so we call meetings, we fast, we rend our garments, we sit *shiva*. . . our heads bowed in sadness, our hands useless, our knees weak. . . . Because over and above the pain we see the weakness, the total inability to rescue or save the victims.

Menachem Ribalow in *Hadoar*, December 4, 1942.

There was really very little that could be done. Germany was in Russia, North Africa, and most of Europe. Allied troops were just beginning to show some signs of success. Americans—even Jewish

Americans—were afraid to receive European refugees, lest those refugees turn out to be spies or saboteurs. Bombing raids aimed at revenge or stopping the transport of Jews to the death camps would mean sending planes away from military targets and delaying the war. Most Jews in America, and in the rest of the free world, were ready to accept the slogan, "rescue through victory."

Then in February 1943, *The New York Times* carried a story claiming that Romanian Jews in concentration camps in Transnistria might be ransomed from the Nazis who were in need of cash. On February 16, a full-page advertisement in the *Times* read:

> For sale to humanity 70,000 Jews. Guaranteed human beings at $50 a piece. Attention America! The Great Rumanian bargain is for this month only.

The advertisement asked those interested in rescuing Jews to send money to the Committee for a Jewish Army—a group first organized to help buy guns and ammunition to be smuggled into Palestine and used against the British. Wise and other American Jewish leaders did not trust this group. They urged American Jews not to send money to the Committee, and said that they would look into the matter of the Romanian Jews.

In March and April, Riegner cabled from Switzerland that there was indeed a possibility of paying the Nazis to release 70,000 Romanian Jews. But the U.S. State Department and the British Foreign Office refused to allow the funds to be transferred. The State Department claimed that any funds sent to Germany would lengthen the war. The British Foreign Office was opposed because of "the difficulty of disposing of any considerable number of Jews should they be released from enemy territory." These decisions were not reached until December 1943. By then, it was already too late for the Jews of Romania.

The March 1 Rally

On March 1, 1943 a "Stop Hitler Now" rally was held in Madison Square Garden. Seventy-five thousand Jews arrived, but the Garden could hold only 20,000. The others stood crowded in the streets listening on loudspeakers. Jewish and non-Jewish leaders spoke, including Stephen S. Wise, Chaim Weizmann, Protestant Episcopal Bishop George Tucker, Mayor Fiorello LaGuardia, Governor Thomas E. Dewey, and Supreme Court Justice William O. Douglas. An 11-point program was announced, calling on the Allies to negotiate for the release of the remaining European Jews; to set up temporary housing for the Jews; to accept more Jewish refugees; to send food to the ghettos and camps; to provide money for rescue efforts; and to punish guilty Germans after the war. Following the rally, the Joint Emergency Committee for Jewish Affairs was organized, and planning for a conference on refugees was speeded up. On the day the conference met in Bermuda, the Warsaw Ghetto Uprising began.

Too Late, Too Late

In London when the fighting in Warsaw began, Shmuel Zygelbojm received a new message from the Warsaw ghetto, asking him to seek help from Jewish leaders. Be warned, the ghetto fighters said,

> Jewish leaders abroad won't be interested. At eleven in the morning you will begin telling them about the anguish of Jews in Poland, but at 1 p.m. they will ask you to halt the narrative so they can have lunch. That is a difference which cannot be bridged. They will go on lunching at their favorite restaurant. So they cannot understand what is happening in Poland.
>
> Cited in Lookstein, *Were We Our Brothers' Keepers?* pp. 156-157.

Since the summer of 1942, Zygelbojm had been trying to get people to listen to him. He knocked at embassy doors, sent telegrams to world leaders, spoke on the radio, talked before large and small audiences. Now his family and friends were dying in the ghetto and he could find no one to help. (During the Warsaw ghetto revolt, Zygelbojm's wife and two small children were killed by the Nazis.) In the end, he gave up hope. He committed suicide on May 12, 1943 by taking poison. In his suicide note, Zygelbojm wrote:

> I cannot be silent. . . . My friends in the Warsaw ghetto died with weapons in their hands in the last heroic battle. It was not my destiny to die together with them but I belong to them and in their mass graves.
>
> By my death I wish to make my final protest against the passivity with which the world is looking on, and permitting the extermination of the Jewish people. . . . Perhaps by my death I shall contribute to breaking down the indifference of those who may now at the last moment rescue the few Polish Jews still alive. . . . I bid farewell to everybody and to everything that was dear to me and that I have loved.
>
> Shmuel Zygelbojm in Morse, *While Six Million Died*, pp. 63-64.

■ When did the world know about the Holocaust? One answer is, the world knew all along. Reports of the mass murder of Jews began in November 1941, even as the killings were beginning! They continued throughout the war. But knowing about mass killings did not mean that Hitler had a program to kill all the Jews.

■ Government officials knew long before the citizens of the free world. Allied spies reported train movements in Poland; killings of Jews in Russia; western Jews being sent to the east to be murdered. In most cases, these reports were filed to be examined after the war was won. In some cases, prejudice against the Jews kept these officials from telling what they knew.

■ Jewish leaders knew of the Holocaust in August 1942 (though they did not fully believe the truth of it until November). Wise promised to keep the terrible secret while the U.S. government checked. Other Jewish leaders made no promises, but also kept silent. Only Shmuel Zygelbojm, the leaders of the Committee for a Jewish Army, and a few other brave souls in Britain and the United States spoke openly of the Final Solution, and most people thought they were exaggerating.

■ The world first heard of the Final Solution in December 1942. It became front-page news for a few days, then faded as the war continued. Nearly everyone in the free world agreed that the way to rescue the Jews of Europe was to win the war. When the armies and the war correspondents reached the gates of the concentration and death camps in 1945, they were horrified. Nothing they had read or heard could have possibly prepared them for what they saw. The peoples of the world knew of the Holocaust but did not believe what they knew.

■ During the war, Jan Karski, a messenger sent by the Polish underground, met U. S. Supreme Court Justice Felix Frankfurter, an American-Jewish leader, at the Polish embassy in Washington.

> [Karski] spoke of shootings, Jews robbed of their possessions, people bundled into trains, gray clouds spiraling from smokestacks, the stench of burning flesh, murders beyond counting . . . the horror of the details. . . .
>
> Frankfurter rose, stared down at Jan Karski. "A man like me talking to a man like you," he said, "must be totally honest. So I am. So I say: I do not believe you." "Felix!" the ambassador cried. "Felix, how can you say such a thing? You know he is saying the truth. . . ."
>
> "I did not say that he's lying," Frankfurter replied. "I said that I don't believe him. There is a difference." Karski said he could not forget the scene, of Frankfurter saying, "My mind, my heart they are made in such a way that I cannot conceive it," and stretching out his arms and crying: "No! No! No!"
>
> Jan Karski paraphrased in Baker, *Brandeis and Frankfurter*, pp. 393-394.

ISSUES

■ The tragic figure of Shmuel Zygel-bojm stands out in this chapter. Escaping from Warsaw, he worked to save the Jews of Poland until his death. When he knew that his friends in the ghetto had died fighting, he committed suicide. The *Jewish Frontier* compared his suicide to a kamikaze pilot's crashing into the deck of a battleship. It was a "suicide dive upon the hardened conscience of the world. Perhaps the steel will be shattered; perhaps the imagination will be stirred."

1. Think back to our discussion of the idea of *kiddush hashem*. Was Zygelbojm's suicide an act that "glorified the Name of God?"

■ A Swiss businessman just returned from a trip to Russia told a ghastly tale. He had been invited by Nazis to witness a mass killing of Jews. He watched as group after group of Jewish men, women, and children were gunned down in cold blood. The memory sickened him. When he returned to Switzerland, he reported what he had seen to the first secretary of the World Council of Churches. Thirty years later, that minister admitted he had known about the Holocaust, but people "did not have the imagination together with the courage to face [such a horror]. It is possible to live in a twilight between knowing and not knowing."

2. Were the people of the free world guilty because they did nothing? Or do you agree with the minister who claimed they were trapped "between knowing and not knowing"?

3. Consider the story of Justice Frankfurter's interview with Jan Karski. And what about government officials who had the facts in front of them? Were they also living in a "twilight" world?

■ In *Pirke Avot* 1:14 the Jewish sage Hillel asked three simple questions: "If I am not for myself, who will be for me? If I am only for myself, what am I? And if not now, when?" The British statesman Edmund Burke (1729-1797) added, "The only thing necessary for the triumph of evil is for good men to do nothing."

4. What do these two quotations mean?

5. What does each of them tell us about the people of the free world during the Holocaust?

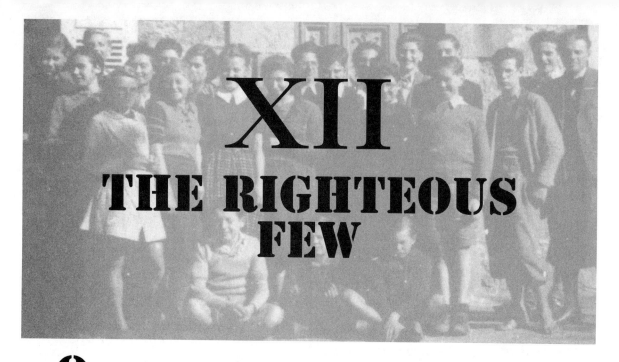

XII
THE RIGHTEOUS FEW

On a radio broadcast made in July 1943, the Jewish congressman Emanuel Celler spoke out against the silence of the U.S. government:

> The problem cries for immediate solution and not for excuses. There are 28 nations fighting Hitler and yet not one, including England and the United States, has said, "We will take Hitler's victims."
>
> Emanuel Celler in Hausner, *Justice in Jerusalem*, p. 238.

Slowly, Celler's voice was joined by many non-Jewish voices. In Britain, some Members of Parliament opposed the policies of their government. Eleanor R. Rathborn, M.P., wrote a pamphlet called *Rescue the Perishing* outlining a practical plan for saving refugees. She chaired the National Committee for Rescue from Nazi Terror. Another Member of Parliament.

> asked whether the [British government's] Home Secretary, seeing a child drowning in a pond, would jump in to save him, or argue that he had saved other children already, or that the [tactical] position made it necessary to be careful of his trousers, or that it was essential first to call a conference of all those others who might equally well jump in—or perhaps he would say that some people do not like children anyway.
>
> A.V. Hill in Hausner, *Justice in Jerusalem*, p. 239.

The pressure to rescue Jews was growing in both Britain and the United States. At one point, the British government offered to accept 5,000 Jewish children from eastern Europe. The Nazis agreed to release the children, provided that the British would release 5,000 German civilians being held in British prisoner of war camps. The British refused, saying that this was not an even exchange—the Jewish children were not British civilians, after all.

By 1943, the number of killings at Auschwitz was reaching 15,000 each day. In June and August of 1944, Jewish leaders called on the Allies to bomb the death camp at Auschwitz. There were good reasons. A bombing raid would bring the killing to a temporary halt, saving tens of thousands of Jewish lives. Also, it was rumored that once a death camp site was discovered, the Nazis abandoned it and moved elsewhere. It would take them years to create another city of death like Auschwitz. (Actually, this was a false rumor: death camps like the one at Auschwitz-Birkenau were never moved.) In addition, the Jewish leaders argued,

Railroad tracks leading to the entrance of Auschwitz-Birkenau.

bombing Auschwitz would be a positive statement, showing that the Allies *did* care about what was happening to the Jews. The Allies refused, repeating their claim that planes were needed to bomb military targets.

The Nazis were well-informed on what was happening in the free world. In his diary, Goebbels noted:

> The question of Jewish persecution is being given top news priority by the English and the Americans and is being handled in high style. Fundamentally, however, I believe both the English and the Americans are happy that we are exterminating the Jewish riffraff.
>
> Josef Goebbels in Hausner, *Justice in Jerusalem*, p. 237.

The Righteous Among the Nations

When governments would not act, when it seemed that the world had turned against the Jews, brave individuals stepped forward to risk their own lives—non-Jews like those who helped to hide the Frank family in Amsterdam. These non-Jews earned the name *hasidei umot haolam,* "the righteous among the nations." Their reasons for helping were many. Anna Semaite was a Lithuanian librarian who helped the people of the Vilna ghetto. She arranged hiding places outside the ghetto for Jewish children, smuggled arms into the ghetto, and smuggled letters and diaries out of the ghetto. She was finally captured by the Gestapo and sent to the camp at Dachau, where she remained until the war ended. She explained:

> When the Germans forced Jews of Vilna into a ghetto, I could no longer go on with my work. I could not remain in my study. I could not eat. I was ashamed that I was not Jewish myself. I had to do something. I realized the danger involved, but it could not be helped. A force much stronger than myself was at work.
>
> Anna Semaite in Friedman, *Their Brothers' Keepers*, p. 22.

Seven nuns in a Benedictine convent near the Vilna railroad terminal provided a hideout and way station for members of the Jewish Fighters' Organization. The nuns made regular visits to the ghetto, the guards never suspecting them. When the Jews needed weapons, the nuns combed the countryside for knives, daggers, bayonets, pistols, guns, and grenades. They smuggled people in and out of Vilna so often that the nunnery sometimes bulged with nuns—many looking suspiciously masculine under their habits.

Mother Maria of Paris headed an underground organization of Greek Orthodox priests that specialized in rescuing Jewish children. Her convent turned out false identification papers and German documents, gave shelter to Jews, and joined with the Catholic underground movement to smuggle Jews out of Paris. She was finally arrested and sent to the women's camp at Ravensbruck, where she continued to show her kindness to the Jewish inmates. She was last seen alive on March 31, 1945, so weak from her work that the guards had to carry her to the gas chambers.

Hiding Jews was not easy. Convents, monasteries, bunkers dug in the earth in forests, mountain caves—these were the safest places to hide. In the cities, neighbors grew suspicious, and rumors sometimes led to capture. Nazis were constantly raiding homes and warehouses, seeking Jews. A non-Jew had to be brave and willing to take risks. Sometimes Jews in hiding had to be moved from place to place. Food had to be provided, and food was scarce everywhere. Sometimes Jewish families were divided among several non-Jewish protectors. Hiding places were often so cramped that Jews had to take turns lying down. The rescuers had to be prepared for nearly anything—a Jew getting sick, a pregnant Jew giving birth, a death among the Jews in hiding. To help their Jewish neighbors, these non-Jews gave up whatever money and supplies they had, sometimes even their lives.

Father Chaillet of Paris rescued Jewish children by sending them to families in the countryside. Another Catholic priest, Alexander Glasberg (a converted Jew), managed to rescue 2,000 Jewish children from French concentration camps, and organized a home for Jewish teenagers. After the war, Glasberg told a Jewish reporter:

> I am not a hero. . . I accomplished no heroic deeds. . . . The two thousand Jews I helped rescue. . .this was a drop in the ocean. Six million Jews were killed. . . . We could have rescued many more if we'd had more money.
>
> Alexander Glasberg in Friedman, *Their Brothers' Keepers*, p. 53.

Raoul Wallenberg

Though individual priests and nuns rescued Jews, the Catholic Pope was silent through most of the war. Many times, Jewish leaders and organizations requested that the Vatican issue an official statement against the Nazis. But the Pope remained silent. Some felt his silence was a sign of anti-Semitism within the Catholic church. Others felt he was silent because he was afraid that, if he spoke out, Catholics in Europe would be treated to their own Final Solution. Whatever the case, in July 1944, he finally broke his silence to join the King of Sweden and the International Red Cross in a joint statement, asking the Hungarians to stop transporting Jews to the death camps. Nearly 450,000 Hungarian Jews were sent to the camps by the middle of 1944, out of a total Jewish population of 800,000.

Raoul Wallenberg, Swedish diplomat and hero who disappeared after the war. It is believed that he was sent to a prison camp by the Russians.

Sweden sent Raoul Wallenberg to Budapest, Hungary, with a list of 700 Jews who had valid passports for Switzerland. Wallenberg set to work saving the remaining Jews of Hungary. Wallenberg built a staff of nearly 400 people, set up 32 safe houses for Jews, and special shelters for 8,000 Jewish children. His staff worked day and night creating false documents for Hungarian Jews, saying that these Jews were "waiting to go to neutral countries." By January 1945, he had given out 20,000 Swedish passports. Once

> He stood on top of a deportation train handing out Swedish papers to all the hands that could reach them, then insisted that the people holding them be allowed off the train. With his own hands, he pulled people out of "death marches" to the Austrian border or brought them bread, soup, and medical supplies in the middle of the night when he had no more passports to give out.
>
> Lester & Werbell, "The Lost Hero,"
> *The New York Times Magazine*, March 30, 1980, p. 39.

Wallenberg kept reminding the Nazis that he was a Swedish diplomat. He even managed to make friends with some of the Nazis, so that they helped him to save Jews. Sometimes he reminded Nazis that, if they did not cooperate, they would be punished after the war. When Russian armies finally captured Budapest in 1945, Wallenberg was arrested by the Russians as a "Nazi collaborator." He was never seen again.

Joop Westerville

A Zionist youth group in Holland organized an underground "railroad" with non-Jews providing a series of hiding places between Holland and Switzerland. But the path was long and only a few children could travel it at any one time. Joachim and Adina Simon looked for a better answer. Joachim began taking small groups of children through France and across the Pyrenees mountains into Spain. This route was still dangerous, but it was easier to cross into Spain than Switzerland. Now, Joachim looked for help so that he could take larger groups.

A member of the Dutch Socialist underground, Joop Westerville, a high school principal, volunteered. Westerville had three children of his own, and a fourth on the way. Thinking nothing of personal danger, he planned for the long trip. Suddenly, Joachim Simon was captured by the Nazis, and then tortured to death. Westerville was forced to go ahead on his own.

Time and again, he led Jewish children across the mountains, leaving them only when they reached the Spanish border. Every day of every trip, he and the children faced danger together. In summer 1944 he was captured by the Nazis and sent to a camp at Vught. The Dutch underground managed to smuggle messages in to tell him to keep up hope—they were planning his rescue. He smuggled messages out. One said:

> I was forced to remain on my feet from Thursday noon until Saturday noon without a break, my hands. . . bound behind my back. I am in a tiny cell in a dark cellar. . . . My daily food ration is four slices of bread and a bottle of tea. . . . They interrogate me, bind

and beat me. . . . Each question is accompanied by blows and kicks. . . . I will not reveal any names to them. I am certain of this. . . . I will remain silent.

Joop Westerville in Freidman, *Their Brothers' Keepers*, pp. 66-67.

An underground messenger carrying plans for Westerville's rescue was captured and killed. Joop Westerville was taken to the woods near Vught and shot.

The Town that Cared

The little French town of Le Chambon sur-Lignon is high in the mountains of south-central France. Winters there are long and cold. Yet this little town became a haven for Jews during the Holocaust. Jewish adults and children were hidden by the villagers and by peasants in the countryside all around the town. Jewish children went to school with non-Jewish children. The

A group of young Jews saved by the town pose outside the Swiss Red Cross building in Le Chambon sur-Lignon.

town even had a pet pig named Adolf. Magda Trocme a town resident, recalled:

> Once when my husband [the Protestant minister of Le Chambon, Andre Trocme] was in Marseilles, he spoke to Burns Chalmers, who was responsible for many of the Quakers' activities on behalf of the inmates of the concentration camps in the south of France. . . . Chalmers said to him, ". . . what we do not have is a place, a village, a house, a place to put people who are hiding, people that we can save. We get people out of the camps, but nobody wants them. It is dangerous to take them. Is your village prepared to do such a thing?
>
> My husband came back to the village and he spoke to the council of the church, and they said, "OK, go ahead." Within minutes, they were willing to help. . . .
>
> Magda Trocme in Rittner & Myers, *Courage to Care*, p. 103.

She went on to explain the actions of the people of Le Chambon, saying:

> We were a bunch of people together. This is not a handicap, but a help. If you have to fight alone, it is more difficult. But we had the support of people we knew, of people who understood without knowing precisely all that they were doing or would be called to do. None of us thought that we were heroes. We were just people trying to do our best. When people read this story, I want them to know that I tried to open my door. I tried to tell people, "Come in, come in." In the end, I would like to say to people, "Remember that in your life there will be lots of circumstances that will need a kind of courage, a kind of decision of your own, not about other people but about yourself."
>
> Magda Trocme in Rittner & Myers, *Courage to Care*, p. 107.

Rescue in Denmark

One of the most remarkable stories of non-Jewish courage is the tale of the rescue of the Jews of Denmark. Germany occupied Denmark in 1940. For two years they tried to force Denmark to adopt anti-Jewish laws. When a Nazi official spoke to King Christian X of Denmark about the "Jewish problem," the King replied, "We have no Jewish problem in our country. The Jews are a part of the Danish nation." In October 1943, the Nazis decided to round up Danish Jews and send them to the death camps. The Danes learned of the intended roundup and the government sent a protest to the Germans. Not waiting for a reply, the Danes made secret arrangements with Sweden and became a nation of rescuers.

Sweden agreed to accept the Jews of Denmark. The problem was how to get them to the shore and then across the 15-mile stretch of water between the two countries. Ignoring all personal risks, the Danes worked together to accomplish this task. Jews were hidden in neighbors' houses, then smuggled in small groups into fishing villages along the water's edge. Years before, the Nazis had seized all large boats, leaving only fishing boats. Now the fishing boats made trip after trip across the channel to Sweden. Over 7,000 Danish Jews—nearly all the Jews of Denmark—were saved in this rescue.

The Danes also refused to make a profit on Jewish property. Rabbi Marcus Melchior of the Copenhagen Synagogue remembered the day he returned to Denmark:

> The people of other countries have let their Jews go before, and, perhaps, they were happy to get rid of them, especially when Jewish homes, property and money were involved. . . . But when we returned, our fellow Danes did say "welcome back." And how they said it—emotionally, with open arms and hearts. Our homes, our businesses, our property and money had been taken care of and returned to us. In most cases we found our homes newly painted, and there were flowers on the table. You cannot imagine how happy it made us feel to be back home. The welcome we received from the King, from everybody, is the most important event in Danish-Jewish history.
>
> Marcus Melchior in Flender, *Rescue in Denmark*, p. 254.

Danish Jews arrive safely in Sweden. Fishing boats and pleasure craft were used by the Danes to ferry the Danish Jews across the channel.

A Desperate Rescue Attempt

For the most part, only non-Jews were in a position to rescue Jews. But, toward the end of war, the British agreed to allow Jews living in Palestine to help. Thirty-two Jewish paratroopers were dropped behind enemy lines in the Balkans—Hungary, Romania, Slovakia, and Italy—with instructions to contact the local underground resistance movements and help get Jews to safety. One of the parachutists was Hannah Senesh. She was chosen because she had been born in Hungary, spoke the language, and had a personal reason for wanting to return—her mother was still there. Senesh and two others landed in Yugoslavia and secretly made contact with the Hungarian resistance fighters. But the Hungarians, learning that the three were Jewish, betrayed them to the Nazis.

One of the three, Joel Nussbacker, escaped by hiding in the French embassy in Budapest. The other two were captured by the Gestapo, tortured, and finally put to death. Hannah Senesh's diary, along with poetry she had written, were found and published after the war. Her name and the story of her heroism became a legend. Nussbacker managed to set up a small Jewish underground. Posing as German officers, he and his group saved several thousand Jewish lives. The parachutists had wanted to save all of Hungary's Jews. Instead, eight of them were killed, many were captured, and some escaped only after being tortured by the Nazis.

Hannah Senesh, best-known of the thirty-two Jewish parachutists dropped behind enemy lines.

A Bitter Truth

The official church organizations of Europe must live with the truth of their silence. Many Protestant churches in Germany even supported the Nazis, while the Catholic church—led by the Vatican—merely refused to speak out. But individual church officials, following their own sense of justice, did rescue Jews. They were joined by many other non-Jewish individuals who worked for Jewish rescue. Sometimes—as in the case of the little town of Le Chambon and the countries of Sweden and Denmark—these rescue operations involved large groups of non-Jews.

The hard fact is that taken altogether, the rescue efforts of nations, of clergy, of individuals—both Jews and non-Jews—saved only a few thousand Jewish lives, while the Nazis managed to take six million. Yet non-Jews who reached out to help have earned a special place of honor in Jewish history.

One of the few Protestant ministers in Germany who opposed the Nazis was Martin Niemoeller, pastor of the Confessing Church. For speaking out against Nazi policies, Niemoeller was arrested, imprisoned, and sent to several concentration camps. Many times he was scheduled for death, but he managed somehow to remain alive to the end of the war. Afterward he explained:

> First they came for the Jews. I was silent. I was not a Jew. Then they came for the Communists. I was silent. I was not a Communist. Then they came for the trade unionists. I was silent. I was not a trade unionist. Then they came for me. There was no one left to speak for me.
>
> Martin Niemoeller in Gutman,
> *Encyclopedia of the Holocaust*, Vol. 3, p. 1061.

Garden of the Righteous, Yad Vashem Martyrs' and Heroes' Memorial, Jerusalem, Israel.

REVIEW

■ When Winston Churchill, Prime Minister of England, heard of the massacres of Jews in eastern Europe, he wrote, "None has suffered more cruelly than the Jew."

> Assuredly in the day of victory the Jew's sufferings and his part in the struggle will not be forgotten. Once again, at the appointed time, he will see vindicated those principles of righteousness which it was the glory of his fathers to proclaim to the world. Once again it will be shown that, though the mills of God grind slowly, yet they grind exceedingly small.
>
> *Winston Churchill* in *The Jewish Chronicle*, November 14, 1941

■ Allied governments failed to act, delaying until it was too late to save the Jews of Europe. But Sweden and Denmark proved by their actions that organized rescues might have saved countless thousands of Jewish lives.

■ Most of the official churches in Europe failed to speak out. But many good Christians acted individually out of charity and sacrifice. Some spoke openly against the Nazi murderers. Others secretly did what they could to rescue Jews. A town like Le Chambon shows what might have been accomplished if more non-Jews had truly loved their neighbors.

■ We are still uncovering heroic stories of rescue. In fact, the State of Israel has taken special notice of *hasidei umot haolam*, "the righteous among the nations." Israel regularly celebrates the work of non-Jews who rescued Jews during the Holocaust years; and a forest planted in Israel is dedicated as a living tribute to their efforts.

■ The many resuce efforts—by Jews and non-Jews, by governments, by churches, by towns—succeeded in saving only a very few Jews from the Nazi whirlwind. Yet this chapter is a reminder that even in the heart of evil—in the midst of the Third Reich—there were people who struggled to do what is right and what is just.

■ A Jewish legend claims that God tolerates evil among human beings because in each generation there are at least thirty-six righteous people. In Hebrew, the number thirty-six is made up of the two letters *lamed* and *vov*, and the thirty-six righteous are called *lamed-vov*niks. No one knows who these people are from one time to another, but according to the legend it is certain that they exist. In a way, all those who risked so much to help the Jews in this tragic hour could truly be called *lamed-vov*niks. They were—each and every one—among the best that humankind has to offer.

ISSUES

■ The term *hasidei umot haolam*, "the righteous among the nations," was first used by the ancient rabbis. It meant any non-Jew who obeyed the seven commandments given by God to Noah. It was thought that such non-Jews had a special place in the World to Come. Mystics believed that all non-Jews who do not hate Israel and who deal justly with Jews are *hasidei umot haolam* [*Zohar*, Exodus, 268a]. Since the Holocaust, the term has been used for those non-Jews who helped Jews escape from Nazi persecutions. These people have received special recognition among Jews, and especially in the State of Israel.

1. From the evidence in this chapter, why do you think that these people helped?

2. Why did other non-Jews not help? Were there good reasons on both sides?

■ The rescue mission of Hannah Senesh and the other Jewish parachutists was mostly a failure. In one of her poems, Hannah Senesh wrote the famous lines, "Blessed is the match consumed in kindling a flame. / Blessed is the heart with strength to stop its beating for honor's sake."

3. Explain the meaning of these lines.

4. Should the parachutists be considered heroes even though their main mission failed? What is a hero?

■ People in Denmark, Sweden, and the French village of LeChambon acted together against the Nazis.

5. Does their action suggest that other groups acted in a cowardly fashion?

6. Why did Alexander Glasberg and Magda Trocme both insist that they were not "heroes"? What did they mean?

■ Consider the different ways in which Christian church groups and individuals acted and spoke throughout this chapter.

7. Do you think things might have been different if all the churches had opposed Hitler? What evidence can you find to support this idea? Look carefully at what was said by Martin Niemoeller.

XIII
A STRUGGLE TO THE DEATH

The Nazis allowed the International Red Cross to "inspect" a concentration camp. The Red Cross inspectors saw what the Nazis arranged for them to see.

> Whenever these visitors arrived, the whole [camp] would be turned upside down. . . . Some places had to be cleaned and made shipshape. Some houses were painted on the outside and large signboards put up, saying, "Central Synagogue," "Ghetto Theater." . . . They even prepared teams of children as if for football games. . . . They put children into small beds with an engraved heart on them, as in a veritable palace. . . . They held rehearsals with children and gave them food, which was ferociously devoured. They had therefore to repeat the rehearsals, for we kept sending them new children each time, so that as many as possible should eat well for once.
>
> Mordechai Ansbacher in Hausner, *Justice in Jerusalem*, p. 158.

The camp at Theresienstadt in Czechoslovakia was a Nazi showcase. To this "model ghetto," they sent well-known Jews, decorated war veterans, some Jewish children, and old people. Of course, Jews were transported out of this camp and sent to real death camps. Jewish prisoners were sometimes tortured or murdered; and some were allowed to starve to death. But the Nazis kept life in Theresienstadt bearable for most prisoners. All this for a very good reason: like many criminals, the Nazis wanted to hide the truth of what they were doing from the rest of the world.

In April 1945, as hope of winning the war dimmed, Himmler ordered Eichmann to release one hundred famous Jews from Theresienstadt. Eichmann delayed. He never got around to setting them free. Even in the "model ghetto," even when it was clear that the war was lost, the Nazis showed little or no mercy to the Jews.

"Arrival at Auschwitz," an ink drawing by Holocaust artist Alfred Kantor.

Final Struggles

The Allied forces landed on the beaches of Normandy, France on June 6, 1944. By midnight, the Germans had lost the battle there, and the Allies had a firm foothold in Europe. In July, Russian troops pushed forward, entering Poland. The Germans retreated before them. By September American troops stood on German soil in the west. Hitler's world was slowly closing in around him.

In one last desperate attack, Hitler sent troops into the Ardennes forest of France, trying to drive a wedge between the American and British armies. This was the Battle of the Bulge, the fiercest and bloodiest battle of World War II. It was over by January 16, 1945. There was no clear victor. But Hitler's army suffered such heavy losses that it would never recover.

A group of smiling Jewish children at Theresienstadt, the "model ghetto." This photograph was probably taken by the Nazis to be used as propaganda.

By early 1945, Allied troops were approaching concentration camps in the east and in the west. The Nazis now began a last-minute attempt to move Jews to central camps like Belsen, Dachau, Buchenwald, Mauthausen, Sachsenhausen, and Ravensbruck, and to cover up the evidence of what they had done. The days of the death marches began. In January, the Nazis abandoned the camp at Auschwitz, leaving many prisoners behind. The Nazis led 54,650 prisoners on a march to the west. Many fell along the roadsides. SS men killed them where they fell.

> On some days there were as many as five hundred shootings. . . .
> We spent the nights in stables or just in the open. . . . Once they
> put us for the night into a very long underground excavation and
> locked the entrance. . . . We were suffocating but they did not open
> to our shouting and knocking. . . . The next day there were a thou-
> sand dead among us.
>
> Aharon Beilin in Hausner, *Justice in Jerusalem*, pp. 174-175.

That same month, a thousand Jewish women were marched southwest from Neusalz. Forty-two days later, only two hundred lived to see Flossenberg. From there, they were sent by train to Belsen.

Sometimes, as the Jews were moved, members of a family found one another. Violette Fintz of Rhodes found her brother in Dachau. She begged him to have the courage to live. But he was already dying from an injury to his leg; and a few days later, he died. Violette was transferred to Belsen, where she miraculously found her sister Miriam.

> Many girls died and we were all thinking that these were our last
> days. My sister Miriam had a very high temperature and she told
> me that if she did not get a little water, she would die there and
> then. . . .

> It is impossible for me to express the scene that was before me: piles of bodies already decomposing, in fact, about a mile of bodies. Shivering at what I had seen, I still managed to go and find some water which I hid [in a tin] inside my dress so no one could see. This relieved my sister a bit.
>
> Many people talk about Auschwitz; it was a horrible camp; but Belsen, no words can describe it. There was no need to work as we were just put there with no food, no water, no anything, eaten by the lice.
>
> Violette Fintz in Gilbert, *The Holocaust*, p. 785.

On some death marches, the Jews could hear the artillery of the Allied armies close behind them. Sometimes Jews were struck by stray Allied bombs, or caught in a crossfire during a battle. But it was not the war that caused them heavy losses of life. It was the continuing cruelty of the Nazis and local anti-Semites.

At the beginning of April, as the Russian armies approached Vienna, 1,300 Jews who had been repairing the bombed Vienna railroad station for the Nazis were marched westward. There was no food for them; they ate whatever they found in the fields. Anyone who fell behind was shot. Only 700 reached the camp at Gusen.

On April 8, the Jews in Buchenwald were marched out, leaving only non-Jewish prisoners of war for the advancing American armies to find. A few Jews, like eight-year-old Israel Lau and his nineteen-year-old brother Naftali, hid for three days. When the Americans entered the camp, Israel Lau was found by an American officer, Rabbi Herschel Schachter. Lau had been hiding in a pile of corpses. When Schachter saw him, he began to cry, then, trying to make the little boy feel safe, started to laugh.

> "How old are you?" he asked Israel Lau, in Yiddish.
>
> "Older than you."
>
> "How can you say that?" asked the rabbi, fearing that the child was deranged.
>
> "You cry and laugh like a little boy," Lau replied, "but I haven't laughed for years and I don't even cry any more. So, tell me, who is older?"
>
> Herschel Schachter, paraphrased in Gilbert, *The Holocaust*, p. 792.

A Jew, a Jew!

On April 13, one of the death marches, made up mainly of survivors from Auschwitz, reached a small town near Belsen. Menachem Weinryb recalls:

> We lay down in a field and several Germans went to consult about what they should do. They returned with a lot of young people from the Hitler Youth and with members of the police force from the town.

Survivors of the Buchenwald concentration camp stare out at their rescuers from the Allied forces.

> They chased us all into a large barn. Since we were five to six thousand people, the wall of the barn collapsed from the pressure of the mass of people, and many of us fled. The Germans poured out petrol and set the barn on fire. Several thousand people were burned alive.
>
> Those of us who had managed to escape lay down in the nearby wood and heard the heart-rending screams of the victims.
>
> Menachem Weinryb in Gilbert, *The Holocaust*, p. 793.

When the British finally entered the camp at Belsen, they found 10,000 unburied bodies, most victims of starvation. There had been no food or water in the camp for nearly five days. Three hundred Jews died of typhus and starvation each day for the first week after the liberation. Two weeks later, 60 a day were still dying. One of those who died was Miriam Fintz. One survivor remembered seeing the British soldiers for the first time.

> Our liberators were well fed and bursting with health, and they moved among our skeletal, tenuous silhouettes like a surge of life. ... They called to one another, whistled cheerfully, then suddenly

> fell silent. . . . How alive they were; they walked quickly, they ran,
> they leapt. All these movements were so easy for them, while a
> single one of them would have taken away our last breath of life!
> These men seemed not to know that one could live in slow motion,
> that energy was something you saved.
>
> Fania Fenelon in Gilbert, The Holocaust, p. 794.

World War II was nearly over, and yet the killing of Jews had not ended. On April 25—the day the Russian and U.S. armies met at Torgau, cutting Germany in half—200 Jewish women were taken from Stutthof to the seashore and shot by the Gestapo. Another 1,500 Jews were loaded on boats to cross the Baltic. Half of these were drowned or shot along the way. That same day, six more Jews were executed by the Gestapo at Cuneo, Italy.

Levi Shalit was liberated by the American troops at Dachau. Hardly believing his good fortune, and testing his new freedom, he walked into a small Austrian town nearby.

> How lovely everything was. How quietly dreamed the little red-
> tiled houses with their little green gardens. . . . Four days before,
> the inhabitants had rushed out at us with axes and blades. Now
> they were invisible. . . .
>
> Here and there American soldiers were on patrol. One came up to
> me, a short fellow with a cheeky face, little more than a child.
>
> "A Jew?"
>
> "A Jew!" I stuttered.
>
> Our arms intertwined and we burbled crazily, "A Jew, a Jew."
>
> Levi Shalit in Gilbert, The Holocaust, pp. 799- 800.

Hitler's End

Adolf Hitler and a few of his most trusted lieutenants went into hiding in a bunker designed and built for him beneath Berlin. In April, when other Nazi leaders were fleeing Berlin and the Allies were surrounding the city, Hitler refused to leave his bunker. In fact, he never left it again alive. On April 30, broken by his defeats, Adolf Hitler shot himself. By his own orders, his body was taken just outside the bunker and burned. Nazi Germany died with him.

One day earlier, Hitler had written a final statement to the German people. Nothing had changed for him, he said. He believed to the end all that he had repeated in speech after speech:

> It is not true that I or anybody else in Germany wanted war in
> 1939. It was wanted and provoked exclusively by those interna-
> tional statesmen who either were of Jewish origin or worked for
> Jewish interests. . . . Disloyalty and betrayal have undermined
> resistance throughout the war. It was therefore not granted to me
> to lead the people to victory. . . . Above all, I enjoin the leaders of

the nation and those under them to uphold the racial laws to their full extent and to oppose mercilessly the universal poisoner of all peoples, International Jewry.

Adolf Hitler in Forman, *Nazism*, p. 113.

For Hitler the war had always been fought against the armies of other nations and against the Jews everywhere within his reach. In his last hours, he continued to urge the struggle against the Jews. The Holocaust was no accident of history; it was first and foremost the plan of a racist who made himself an emperor. But the murder of six million people could not be carried out by one man alone. Thousands of Germans and thousands of people in occupied countries had taken part.

Jewish concentration camp survivors at Buchenwald. Most survivors weighed between 50% and 60% of their normal body weight and had shrunk to less than their average height. Many could not lift themselves from their shelf-like beds. Among the survivors in this photograph is Elie Wiesel, who would later win the Nobel Peace Prize.

On one of the death marches, word was received that Hitler had died. The SS men whispered it to one another, and it was overheard by the Jews. Within moments, the news spread through the ranks of the Jewish marchers. One of the Jews started dancing, chanting, "I have out-lived the fiend! My heart is full of joy."

> One of the German guards lifted his gun, took aim. We saw the "Joker" lift his arms again, stand up, turn around, surprised (didn't they understand, hadn't they heard, that the Monster was dead?) and, like a puppet when its strings are cut, collapse into a heap.
>
> Michael Etkind in Gilbert, *The Holocaust*, p. 805.

Jewish children who had spent the war hidden in convents, monaster-ies, and Christian homes line up in front of a Jewish children's home in lower Silesia in November, 1946.

Not Just Jews

No record of the Holocaust would be complete without noting that the Jews were not the only ones who suffered Nazi cruelty. Everywhere they ruled, the Nazis shot unarmed civilians—Czechs, Russians, Poles, Greeks, Russians, and others. Nazis tortured and murdered, by shooting and starvation, several million Russian prisoners-of-war. Other groups besides Jews were also singled out for special Nazi treatment: Nearly 250,000 gypsies were murdered. Homosexuals were murdered by the thousands. Tens of thousands of mentally and physically handicapped people fell to Nazi cruelty. Millions of non-Jews were murdered by the Nazis.

Hitler had tried to destroy many groups—the mentally and physically handicapped, gypsies, Jehovah's Witnesses, and homosexuals. But the group he hated most from beginning to end was the Jews. The Nazis used the entire machinery of the German state—police, railroads, factories, soldiers, propaganda, and government—to wipe out all Jewish life in Europe. Against this, the Jews of Europe had only one real weapon: to survive. As Gerda Klein, a survivor herself, wrote, "It seemed almost a luxury to die, to go to sleep and never wake up again." Yet it was a duty to live, a solemn duty.

The *Exodus* was filled with refugees being smuggled to Palestine in 1947. Captured by the British, the Jews were sent back to displaced persons camps inside Germany. People all over the world were shocked at this brutal treatment of the Jewish survivors.

There Was No Homecoming

Even when the war was over, the Jewish struggle to survive continued. The German armies surrendered on May 8. Yet the remaining Jews of Europe were still not safe. Some tried to return home, hoping to live in peace. But this was seldom possible. On August 20—anti-Jewish riots broke out in Cracow. On October 25—Jews were attacked in Sosnowiec. On November 19—rioting was directed against Jews in Lublin.

Some Polish underground groups actually continued to specialize in killing Jews! In the first seven months after the war, 350 Jews were killed on Polish soil, not one of them by a German. In Radom, a hospital for Jewish orphans was attacked. The British ambassador in Warsaw, Poland reported that anyone who even looked Jewish was in danger.

The worst incident happened on July 4, 1946 in Kielce. Rumors spread that the Jews had kidnapped a Christian child. The building of the Jewish Committee was invaded. Jews were dragged from their homes into the streets. They were shot, stoned to death, or killed with axes and blunt instruments. Forty-two Jews died in the Kielce pogrom. Hearing of the pogrom, 100,000 Jews fled Poland, Hungary, and Czechoslovakia.

Anti-Semitism continued to haunt the survivors in Germany, Lithuania, Hungary, Czechoslovakia, and the Ukraine. There was no way for those who had suffered so much to come "home." They no longer had a home in Europe, and few nations outside of Europe were open to them.

Raising the flag of the new State of Israel at the United Nations.

REVIEW

■ In fact, Jews who survived the war no longer had a home. They crowded into the American zone, hoping to find a way to America or Palestine. But Palestine was still closed. The British had promised the Arabs that they would keep Jewish immigration at a minimum. And the United States, despite the efforts of its new president Harry S Truman, held to its quota system, admitting very few Jews.

■ The Zionist Jews of Palestine organized an underground movement—buying, renting, and refitting old ships to smuggle Jewish refugees into Palestine. The struggle against the British was resolved only on November 29, 1947, when the United Nations voted to create the Jewish state. The State of Israel was declared on May 14, 1948. By 1951, two-thirds of the survivors of the Holocaust had been settled in Israel.

■ Possibly the State of Israel would have been established had there been no Holocaust. The Holocaust, and the need to find a home for Holocaust survivors, certainly speeded up the establishment of the State. But imagine how much richer—phys-ically and spiritually—the new State would have been if there had been no Holocaust, if the eight million Jews of Europe could have guided the orderly development of the new nation. Imagine the talents that were lost, the great tradition cut off in full bloom, the resources and heritage that could have been employed in the building of Israel.

■ All this was lost forever in the Holocaust. The few remaining Jews of Europe enriched the lives of the communities they joined—Palestine, France, Britain, Latin America, Australia, Canada, and the United States. But they never recovered from the horrors of the past. They never forgot that they had been abandoned to die. As the Yiddish poet Edward Yashinsky wrote:

> Fear not your enemies, for they can only kill you. Fear not your friends, for they can only betray you. Fear only the indifferent, who permit the killers and betrayers to walk safely on the earth.
>
> Edward Yashinsky in Lookstein, *Were We Our Brothers' Keepers?* p. 217.

ISSUES

■ The Nazi leaders in charge of the "Final Solution of the Jewish Questions—Hitler, Heydrich, Himmler, Eichmann, Hoess, and others—believed that they were at war against the Jews, just as the German generals believed that they were at war with the Allies. Himmler once defined "true wars" as "wars between races." He said that such wars were fought "until one side or the other is eliminated without trace." Even when the Allies were clearly winning the war against Germany, the Nazis continued to use valuable trains and equipment in the other war, the war against the Jews. But the Holocaust historian Lucy Dawidowicz pointed out that the Nazis had to be

> truly mad [to have] believed that it was war they were waging against the Jews. For the Jews were a civilian population, dispersed among the European nations, having no country and no political power, and consequently none of the resources that even small nations could muster for war.
>
> Dawidowicz,
> *The War Against the Jews*, p. 223

1. Why did Nazis continue to murder Jews even when it was clear that the Allies were about to win the war?

2. Why didn't anti-Semitism come to an end in Europe after the war was over?

3. Is there anti-Semitism in Europe today?

■ Two thirds of the Jewish population of Europe perished in the Holocaust. This meant that nearly one third of them could have chosen to return home when Germany was defeated. Most of them chose not to go back to their old homes.

4. What happened to those who did try to return to their old homes?

5. Why did most Jews choose to start their lives in new places? What kept them from returning home?

6. Was it only human beings that the Nazis destroyed in the Holocaust?

■ There were also many reasons why the peoples of countries like Germany, Poland, Austria, Hungary, Greece, and Romania were not eager to have one third of their former Jewish neighbors return.

7. From what you have read and studied thus far, can you give some of the reasons?

8. Contrast what happened to the remaining Jews of Poland after the war with the story of how Danish Jews returned home (see Chapter 12). What are the major differences? What similarities exist?

■ Many students of the Holocaust find this period—the time of the death marches and the displaced persons' camps—the most distressing part of studying the Holocaust.

9. What event in this chapter surprised you the most? Which event or events depressed you the most? Which events gave you the most pleasure?

XIV
WAR CRIMES AND PUNISHMENT

On December 17, 1942, eleven Allied governments promised that the Nazis would be brought to justice after the war (see Chapter 11). Justice seems a simple idea—guilty persons must be punished in a way that is equal to their crimes. The book of Exodus [21:23-24] states "the penalty shall be life for life, eye for eye, tooth for tooth." The Latin name for this law is *lex talionis*, "law of the talon" (a "talon" is the claw of a bird or animal). The law plainly describes the revenge common among beasts. But putting simple justice into everyday human terms is not simple.

The ancient Rabbis had struggled with the *lex talionis*. First, they pointed out, it is a law and not a decree for private revenge—punishment must be pronounced by a judge. Second, the law states "life for life," but no two lives are ever really equal. If the crime is not intentional murder, then the law means the murderer must make fair compensation. If I put out your eye accidentally, the court does not put out my eye, but requires me to pay you a sum of money. How much is your eye worth? In the Mishnah, the Rabbis ruled the amount must "pay for injury and pain inflicted, for healing and loss of time, and for indignity suffered."

The London Charter

When the Allies decided to bring guilty Nazis to justice, they faced an enormous task. The Nazis' crime was the intentional murder of millions of people. The murder of millions had been made "legal" under Hitler. So it was not just individuals, but an entire government or nation that had turned renegade. But the death of millions of Germans would not be *fair compensation*. And, in a practical sense, each individual would first have to be given a fair trial—and that was an impossible task. As always, the court would have to find a middle ground between simple justice and legal justice.

Meeting in London on August 8, 1945, the Allies chartered a court to bring war criminals to justice. The Charter called for an International Military Tribunal, made up of four judges and four teams of attorneys representing the major Allied nations—France, Britain, Russia, and the United States. Article 61 of the Charter said:

> The Tribunal. . . shall have the power to try and punish persons who, acting in the interests of the European Axis countries, whether as individuals or as members of organizations, committed any of the following crimes: a) crimes against peace; b) war crimes; c) crimes against humanity.
>
> Cited in Sherwin & Ament, *Encountering the Holocaust*, p. 148.

The Allied Commander, General Dwight D. Eisenhower—accompanied by generals Patton and Bradley—examines the corpses of Jewish victims at Ohrduf, May, 1945. The Allies found evidence of war crimes in every sector of their occupation.

Of these three crimes, "war crimes" was the best defined in a legal sense. The Charter explained:

> Sec. 6b): War crimes: namely, violations of the laws or customs of war. . . . murder, ill-treatment or deportation to slave labor or for any other purpose of civilian populations of or in occupied territory. . . .
>
> Cited in Sherwin & Ament, *Encountering the Holocaust*, p. 150.

The Charter also defined the meaning of "crimes against humanity":

> Sec. 6c): Crimes against humanity, namely, murder, extermination, enslavement, deportation, and other inhumane acts committed against any civilian population, before or during the war, or persecutions on political, racial, or religious grounds in execution of or in connection with any crime within the jurisdiction of the Tribunal, whether or not in violation of the domestic law of the country where perpetrated.
>
> Cited in Sherwin & Ament, *Encountering the Holocaust*, p. 150.

A major difference between "war crimes" and "crimes against humanity" was that "war crimes" could be committed only during a war, while "crimes against humanity" could be committed before or during a war.

The definition of "crimes against humanity" was based on a *precedent*, an earlier case or trial. The Allied precedent was the massacre, during World War I, of Armenians in Turkey. This massacre had been carried out by the Turkish government. At that time, the governments of France, Great Britain, and Russia declared that the Armenian massacres were "crimes against humanity and civilization," and that all members of the Turkish government would be held responsible. In the same way, the Nazis could now be held responsible.

The trials were held in Nuremberg, Germany, beginning on November 20, 1945. They continued through 403 court sessions. Over one hundred thousand captured German documents were studied as the lawyers prepared for the trials. The official English-language record of the trials fills forty-two large volumes. The Nuremberg trials were the largest war crimes trials in history, but not the first. As with "crimes against humanity," there were precedents for "war crimes" trials.

Earlier War Crimes Trials

Before Nuremberg, the most famous war crimes trial of modern times took place at the end of the American Civil War. It was the trial of Captain Henry Wirts, a Confederate officer who had commanded the prison camp at Andersonville, Georgia. This camp had a reputation for starvation and cruelty that was not equaled until Hitler's time. Wirts was accused of the deaths of several thousand Yankee prisoners of war. He was tried by a military court, convicted, and hanged.

Another major war crimes trial took place after World War I. Most nations had agreed to certain "laws of warfare" drawn up in 1899 and in 1907. And two Geneva Conventions, in 1864 and 1906, had also laid down international laws regarding the conduct of war. In signing the Treaty of Versailles (see Chapter 6), Germany admitted to breaking some of these laws and agreed to turn over the guilty parties to stand trial. The Allies drew up a list of 900 names, but politics and time wore the list down. Only thirteen Germans were actually brought to trial, the court and judges were German, and six of the thirteen were set free.

The Nuremberg Trial

The first job facing the court at Nuremberg was to decide who should be tried. Though Hitler and a few others had taken their own lives, most of the top Nazi leaders had been captured by the Allies. Hundreds of names of accused Nazis were brought before the court. The International Military Tribunal decided to try only twenty-four of the central leaders of the Nazi Party. The job of local trials was turned over to the Allied powers who now occupied parts of Germany and to those countries in which war crimes had taken place. To defend the Nazi officers, the Tribunal hired well-respected lawyers. The Nazis could choose among them or request any other lawyer.

In the trials, the prosecution tried to show that the Nazis had planned the war (a crime against peace). They claimed that Nazis like Hermann Goering, Joachim von Ribbentrop, Hans Frank (who had been Governor General of Nazi-occupied Poland), Julius Streicher, and Albert Speer had planned to conquer the world if they could. As a minor part of its case, the prosecution presented witnesses and documents that told the story of the Holocaust. The defense lawyers could not claim that the Holocaust had never happened—there was too much evidence—so they made their case on other issues.

The defense first claimed that the Tribunal had no legal authority. They said the court was just a way for the Allies to take "revenge"; that it was a "show trial" to justify executing individual Nazis, when really it was the government of Nazi Germany that was at fault. These Nazi leaders had only been "following orders." But the judges declared:

> That international law imposes duties and liabilities upon individuals as well as upon States... Crimes against international law are committed by men, not by abstract entities [such as a government or political party], and only by punishing individuals who commit such crimes can... international law be enforced.
>
> Sherwin & Ament, *Encountering the Holocaust*, p. 154.

The accused Nazi war criminals in the dock during the Nuremberg trials: Hermann Goering, Rudolf Hess, Joachim von Ribbentrop, Wilhelm Keitel, Ernst Kaltenbrunner, Alfred Rosenberg, Hans Frank, Wilhelm Frick, Julius Streicher, Walter Funk, Hjalmar Schacht, Karl Doenitz, Erich Raeder, Baldur von Schirach, Fritz Sauckel, Alfred Jodl, Franz von Papen, Arthur Seyss-Inquart, Albert Speer, Constantin von Neurath, Hans Fritzsche.

The judges said that all people are aware of certain basic laws such as the law against murder, the law against enslavement, and the law against extermination. Duty to these human laws comes before duty to any state or nation, and a person will not be forgiven for "following orders" in violation of these laws. In fact, the higher a person is in military or governmental authority, the greater his or her accountability.

The defense had one more argument: the *Fuhrer-prinzip*, the Nazi "leadership principal." Hitler had been the absolute dictator, the Fuhrer, of Nazi Germany. All orders given in Germany were Hitler's orders, and the punishment for not obeying was death. All other Nazis were innocent; only Hitler could be held responsible.

The Tribunal rejected this argument. The judges stated:

> It was also submitted on behalf of most of these defendants that . . . they were acting under the orders of Hitler. . . . That a soldier was ordered to kill or torture in violation of the international law of war has never been recognized as a defense to such acts of brutality.
>
> Hausner, *Justice in Jerusalem*, p. 396.

Amazingly enough, the laws of Nazi Germany itself agreed with this ruling. Article 47 of the German Military Law stated that "no obedience was due to an order that called for the performance of a crime." This law applied to the SS as well as the German army.

When the verdicts were handed down, three men were set free. Although they had been part of the leadership, the court did not think they were guilty of crimes against humanity. Nineteen men were found guilty. Twelve were sentenced to hanging, including several who were pointed out as having had a hand in the murder of Jews: Goering, Streicher, Frank, Alfred Rosenberg (who had been in charge of Jews in the eastern territories), and Arthur

Seyss-Inquart (an Austrian in charge of Jews in the Netherlands). The Tribunal had toiled to be fair. And the Nuremberg trials set a precedent in moral history, affirming that individuals are always responsible for their actions—in war time as well as in times of peace.

After the Nuremberg Trials

The Nuremberg trials were long—lasting nearly a year. The trials were front-page news at first, but as time went on, news of the trials moved to the inside pages of the world press.

> The American public's attention did not stay riveted on the [Nuremberg] trial throughout its whole course. The years 1945-46 marked the transition from war to peace and filled the lives of most Americans with complex problems and new interests. The trial had to compete. . . with the first new American automobiles manufactured in four years. The trial could not win such a contest.
>
> Bradley Smith, *Reaching Judgement at Nuremberg*, pp. xiii-xiv.

Afterward, there were dozens of smaller trials of other Nazi war criminals. Some of these men had been in charge of ghettos, concentration camps, or death camps. There were trials of Nazi doctors who had used Jews in unspeakable experiments. And there were trials of officers and leaders of the *Einsatzgruppen*. Lawyers, statesmen, and judges realized that these trials were important—indeed, history making—but most people were busy returning to normal life. The world paid little attention as the story of the Holocaust was told in one small trial after another. Because the Holocaust had played a very small part in the Nuremberg trials, many people had hardly ever heard of it.

Thus, for many more years, the world knew little about the "Final Solution." Few people were aware of the Nazi murder of the gypsies; the murder of Russian, Polish, and Slav civilians; the "euthanasia" programs directed at the sick, the lame, the physically deformed, and the mentally handicapped. For more than a decade after the war, the Holocaust was barely mentioned in history courses in German schools and universities.

But times were changing. Television was soon the new mass medium. Soon the Jews would use the media—television, radio, magazines, and newspapers—not for propaganda, but to tell the world the truth about what happened in the Holocaust.

The Eichmann Trial

In the confusion following the war, some high-ranking Nazis escaped from the Allies. The less important Nazis usually remained in Europe. Top officials, however, found Allied-occupied Europe too dangerous for them; many fled. Two Nazi-hunters—Simon Wiesenthal and Tuviah Friedman—continued to keep files on Nazi criminals. When they located former Nazis, they turned them in to governments in Europe for trial. But as time passed, European governments were less eager to stir up old troubles, and the number of trials dwindled. Many Nazi criminals remained at large.

The Eichmann Trial. At right, prosecuting attorney Gideon Hausner faces the prisoner. Eichmann's face showed no emotion as the horrors of the Holocaust were reviewed in great detail.

In 1948, a special section of the Israeli secret service was organized to find Nazis and bring them to justice. In 1950, the State of Israel passed the "Law of Judging Nazi Criminals and Their Helpers." This law spoke of Israel's right—on behalf of the six million Jews who had died—to bring former Nazis to trial in the Jewish state.

Unfortunately, ex-Nazis were actually welcomed in many places, especially in South America. Informing one of these governments that an ex-Nazi was hiding in its country served no real purpose. The Nazi was not turned over to Israel, and he would often escape to a new hiding place. Therefore, when the Israeli secret service located Adolf Eichmann living under a new identity in Argentina, they kidnapped him and brought him to Israel to stand trial under the 1950 law.

On May 23, 1960, the prime minister of Israel, David Ben-Gurion, told the Israeli *Knesset* (parliament) that Eichmann had been captured, was in Israel, and would face trial. It seemed that the imagination of the world was captured along with Eichmann. Suddenly, all eyes were on Jerusalem.

Adolf Eichmann listens as the court in Jerusalem declares him guilty.

As the trial unfolded, the whole story of the Holocaust and the "Final Solution" came at last to the public eye. For his own protection, Israel built a bulletproof glass booth from which Eichmann watched and listened. Eichmann chose his own lawyer, a German attorney who was paid by the State of Israel.

Eichmann was the Nazi most directly in charge of the Holocaust. In an interview, some years before, he said that he still believed that

> the battlefields of this war were the destruction camps. . . Had we killed all of [the Jews], I would be happy and say, all right, we managed to destroy an enemy.
>
> Adolf Eichmann in Hausner, *Justice in Jerusalem*, pp. 10-11.

During the war, he had said:

> I will jump with joy into my grave in the knowledge that I drag with me millions of Jews.
>
> Adolf Eichmann in Hausner, *Justice in Jerusalem*, pp. 267.

At Nuremberg, one of Eichmann's closest co-workers had called him "a coward at heart," saying:

> his character and personality were important factors in carrying out measures against the Jews. . . . Eichmann was very cynical in his attitude toward the Jewish question. He gave no indication of any human feeling toward these people. He was not immoral, he was amoral and completely ice-cold in his attitude.
>
> Dieter Wisliceny in Hausner, *Justice in Jerusalem*, p. 13.

As the facts of the Holocaust were presented, the world watched the trial on televisions, listened on radios, and read newspaper and magazine accounts. Eichmann was found guilty, sentenced to die, and hanged. His ashes were scattered over the Mediterranean Sea outside Israeli waters.

Following the trial, more Holocaust survivors came forward to tell their own personal stories of what had happened. More scholars turned to the work of studying the documents of the Holocaust. More historians wrote accounts of the Holocaust. Thousands of captured documents that had barely been touched since the end of the war were translated and read for the first time. Textbooks—even textbooks in Germany—were rewritten to include the Holocaust. Encyclopedias made space for special articles on the Holocaust. At last, the truth was well known.

Nazis in the United States

Not all Nazis escaped to South America. Immediately after the war, the U.S. government imported ex-Nazi scientists to work in the U.S. space program. The Russians also recruited ex-Nazi scientists to work in their space and weapons development programs. In 1948, the United States eased the immigrant quota system to allow World War II refugees from Europe to come to America. By 1952, some 400,000 Europeans, many of them Jews, arrived. With so many immigrants to process, records were not carefully checked, and Nazis could enter by just inventing an imaginary past and presenting a few false papers.

The hunt for Nazi war criminals in the United States began very slowly. Many of the hunters came to believe that the Nazis had "friends in high places," perhaps even in the government. Ex-Nazis also seemed to have an endless supply of cash. Some of the hunters believed that they were being supported by secret Nazi networks. In the 1960s, the World Jewish Congress (WJC) compiled a list of 59 names and addresses of known Nazi war criminals living in America. The list was given to the U.S. Immigration and Naturalization Service. Files were opened on these people, and investigations were begun. But very little action was taken. By the mid-1970s, seventeen of the persons on the WJC list had died of natural causes.

In 1974, Elizabeth Holtzman, a member of Congress, demanded that the Justice Department report on Nazi investigations. Why were Nazi criminals not being deported to stand trial for their crimes? Her campaign led to the creation of a special investigating unit. The Office of Special Investigations has since researched hundreds of cases. Twenty cases have been brought to trial. One ex-Nazi was living in Detroit, posing as a bishop in the Catholic church! During the war, this "bishop" served as commandant of the Romanian Iron Guard, responsible for the death of 4,000 Jews. Another Nazi criminal was a county official in New Jersey, though he had once been an officer in the murderous *Einsatzgruppen*. Another was a Long Island housewife who had once been a guard at the Maidanek concentration camp. She had hanged a girl for sport, and beat another to death with a whip.

How many more Nazi criminals still live peacefully in the United States? It is difficult to know. Yet, with the passage of time, bringing them to justice becomes a race against death.

The American armies were so horrified by the remains of the Holocaust that they forced Germans to walk past them, hoping to impress
them with the memory of what the Nazis had done.

REVIEW

■ Justice is a difficult thing to achieve. In the case of the Holocaust, it is impossible even to think of achieving it. Why bother hunting the war criminals and turning them over to governments which have little interest in putting them on trial? Even when they are convicted and imprisoned for life or hanged, does it make any difference?

One answer may be found in the words of an American journalist, written just after the Eichmann trial:

> The trial was essential, to every human being now alive, and to all who follow us. . . . No one who tries to understand our times, now or in the future, can overlook this documentation of a way of life and death which will stain our century forever. No one will see the complete dimension of twentieth-century men—and that includes all of us, I insist—without studying the Eichmann trial.
>
> Martha Gellhorn in Hausner, *Justice in Jerusalem*, p. 472.

■ The chapters in this unit have spoken of resistance, rescue, and justice. But what about revenge? Weren't there Jews in Europe who wanted to take revenge for what had been done to them and their families? It would seem abnormal if *none* of the Jewish survivors wanted revenge.

■ In fact there were a handful of Jews who organized themselves into small revenge squads and took the law into their own hands. They did not wait for trials or juries. They hunted down guards and commanders of concentration death camps. They trailed members of the Gestapo and Nazi officers who had tortured and murdered Jews. And they searched for Nazi doctors who had performed cruel experiments on Jews. They knew these people to be guilty of murder, and when the hunters found them, they killed them. But the madness passed quickly—in all, we know of only a few dozen Nazis who were put to death by these revenge squads. And some of the Jews on these squads felt so badly about committing murder that they later committed suicide.

■ The remarkable thing about the vast majority of Jewish survivors was that they managed to keep their humanity, even though the world they lived in had gone mad all around them. They dreamed of revenge, of course—they were only human. But they turned their talents to making new lives for themselves and for their remaining relatives. The victory of the Jews of Europe was not in surviving the Holocaust, but in surviving it with dignity and humanity. The ultimate victory against the Nazi whirlwind was the survival of Judaism and the Jewish spirit.

ISSUES

The State of Israel normally has no death penalty. Only when a person is found guilty under the Law of Judging Nazi Criminals and Their Helpers is the death penalty allowed. Although the Torah calls for death as a punishment for many laws, the death penalty was extremely rare in ancient Israel. The Talmud states that a Sanhedrin [court] which executed a person once in seven years was called destructive. Rabbi Eleazar b. Azariah said, "Once in seventy years." Rabbis Tarphon and Akiba said, "If we were members of a Sanhedrin, never would a person be put to death."

1. How do you feel about the death penalty?

2. Is the case of the Nazi war criminal a special case? Explain.

The value of justice is very important in the Jewish tradition. The Midrash says, "Do not sneer at justice, for it is one of the three feet of the world, for the sages taught that the world stands on three things: justice, truth, and peace. Therefore consider that if you pervert justice, you shake the world. . . ."

3. In what way do trials like the Nuremberg trials, the Eichmann trial, and the many Nazi war crimes trials promote justice in the world?

4. What is the difference between justice and revenge?

So much time has passed since the end of World War II that most of the Nazi war criminals still at large are old. Many of them have already died; and many may be near death.

5. Should the hunters stop hunting?

Many Jews refused for a long time to buy or use products made by German industries or to visit Germany.

6. Were they right to blame the entire German nation for the Holocaust? If so, has the time come to forgive Germany? (If this issue interests you, you may wish to read the book, *The Sunflower*, by Simon Wiesenthal.)

YAD VASHEM MEMORIAL
JERUSALEM, ISRAEL

Postscript:

REMEMBERING THE HOLOCAUST

We have examined some of the photographs, the documents, the stories—the evidence—of the Holocaust. But what we have seen and read here is only a small portion of the record of what happened. There are six million individual stories, and many of them we will never be able to know.

It is shocking to look at photographs of the death camps and ovens. Didn't the people who used these tools know what they were doing? That it was savage and barbaric? Didn't the German people, especially those near the ghettos and the camps, understand that they were instruments of torture and murder—of evil? Why did they fail to do anything? Why did they fail to at least speak out?

The clarity with which we see the Holocaust today hides an important point about why we must study the Holocaust. Remember, always remember, that during the 1933-45 few people spoke out against the evil that was spreading through Germany and Europe. In Germany, elsewhere in Europe, and in America, people were guilty of silence in the face of great evil. And silence has a price.

In truth, there were many good people in Germany, and around the world. When Hitler first appeared, he promised Germans better times, relief from their economic suffering, and he gave them new pride in being German. So the German people accepted his policies, including those of repression of the Jews. But as the evil grew they remained silent, and soon it was too late.

Most Germans were guilty of being silent; for this silence, the nation paid a heavy price. Many Germans died and the country was left in ruins at the end of World War II. Most Germans were ashamed to admit that they had ever supported Hitler, the Nazis, or anti-Semitism.

One of the reasons for the ease with which Hitler conquered Europe was the lack of outrage around the world. Many, those next door to the concentration camps and those in other parts of the world, closed their eyes and their minds to the horror that they knew existed. As a result, millions of people went to silent deaths with little hope of being remembered. Individual lives, and whole families, would be forgotten, lost in the number six million.

But it is our obligation to remember the people who died not as six million but as one, and one, and one. It is the obligation of those who survive, and those who remember, to speak out and preserve the memory of the victims of the Holocaust. We must do so because the victims demand it, those still living and those who left written words which survived their death:

> Everything depends on who...writes the history of this period. History is usually written by the victor.... Their every word will be taken for gospel. Or they may wipe out our memory altogether as if we had never existed, as if there had never been a Polish Jewry, a Ghetto in Warsaw, a Maidanek [concentration camp]. Not even a dog will howl for us.
>
> Leon Wells, The Janowska Road, p. 211

Religious thinkers—Jewish and non-Jewish—have struggled with another enduring question of the Holocaust: Where was God? How could a just and compassionate God allow the horrors of Auschwitz to occur? How can we believe in god once we learn of the Holocaust?

Some, like Richard Rubenstein, have said that "God is dead" or that God no longer cares about the fate of human beings. Others, such as Emil Fackenheim, conclude that the Holocaust has created an additional commandment that the Jewish people must survive and must not grant Hitler "posthumous victories." Most agree that the Holocaust is the responsibility of human beings, not God. The novelist Meyer Levin concluded that to believe in God one must believe the Holocaust is the responsibility of humanity:

> God has given us free will. . . to choose between good and evil. . . God could not therefore permit himself to interfere in man's actions, for then there would be an end to free will . . . This, and only this,. . . can give us back a belief in God—in a compassionate, torn, and sorrowing God who gave us free will out of love, and having forbidden himself to interfere, must behold in agony what we do with our freedom.

The Bible tells the famous story of the first murder. Cain rose up against his brother Abel in the field and killed him. God asked Cain, "Where is your brother Abel? and Cain answered with the question, "Am I my brother's keeper?" The answer is yes—we are all responsible for watching over one another. Whenever a person is murdered, we must all answer the question, "Why were we not better keepers?"

VALLEY OF THE DESTROYED COMMUNITIES
YAD VASHEM MEMORIAL
JERUSALEM, ISRAEL

A HOLOCAUST CHRONOLOGY

1933

JANUARY 30   Hitler becomes Chancellor of Germany.

FEBRUARY 28   *Reichstag* fire set by Nazis. Constitution of Germany is suspended. Hitler is given "emergency" powers.

MARCH 10   First concentration camp set up at Dachau.

APRIL 1   Hitler orders a one-day boycott of Jewish shops.

APRIL 7   first anti-Jewish law passed in Germany.

1934

FEBRUARY 7   Hitler's Defense Council declares its intention to prepare for war.

JUNE 30   Hitler consolidates power by executing Ernst Roehm and several other Nazi leaders.

AUGUST 3   Hitler declares himself both President and Chancellor of Germany.

1935

SEPTEMBER 15   First Nuremberg laws passed. German Jews lose their citizenship.

NOVEMBER 14   Nazis define a "Jew" as anyone with three Jewish grandparents, or anyone with two Jewish grandparents who claims to be Jewish.

1937

JULY 2   Many Jewish students ordered to leave German schools and universities.

JULY 19   Buchenwald concentration camp set up.

NOVEMBER 16   Jewish passports are declared invalid for foreign travel.

1938

MARCH 12   Germany takes over Austria. All anti-Jewish laws are enforced in Austria.

OCTOBER 28   15,000 Jews are forced at gunpoint to cross the border into Poland.

NOVEMBER 9   *Kristallnacht* begins, resulting in enormous destruction to Jewish property in Germany.

NOVEMBER 15   All Jewish students are expelled from German schools.

1939

AUGUST 23   Russia and Germany sign a non-aggression pact.

SEPTEMBER 1   Germany declares war on Poland.

SEPTEMBER 3   World War II begins.

OCTOBER 12   First trainload of Austrian Jews sent to camps in Poland.

NOVEMBER 23   All Polish Jews ordered to wear a yellow badge imprinted with a Star of David.

NOVEMBER 28   First ghetto set up in Poland at Protrkow.

1940

FEBRUARY 12   First time that German Jews are sent to concentration camps.

APRIL 9   Germans occupy Denmark.

MAY 10   Germany invades Holland, Belgium, and France.

MAY 20   Auschwitz concentration camp set up.

JUNE 22   France surrenders to Germany.

SEPTEMBER 27   Japan joins Germany and Italy in Axis Powers.

OCTOBER 2   Warsaw ghetto set up.

NOVEMBER 20-24   Hungary, Romania, and Slovakia join the Axis Powers.

1941

MARCH   Adolf Eichmann appointed head of Gestapo section for Jewish affairs.

APRIL   Germany occupies Greece and Yugoslavia.

JUNE 22   Germany invades Russia.

JUNE-DECEMBER   *Einsatzgruppen* begin mass murder of eastern European Jewry.

SEPTEMBER 1   German Jews ordered to wear the yellow badge.

SEPTEMBER 28-29   Massacre of 35,000 Jews at Babi Yar, near Kiev.

OCTOBER 14   Mass deportation of Jews to concentration camps begins. Birkenau camp opened as extermination camp.

OCTOBER 23   Massacre of 19,000 Jews in Odessa.

DECEMBER 7   Japanese attack Pearl Harbor. United States joins the Allied Powers.

1942

JANUARY 20   Plans for the "Final Solution of the Jewish Problem" discussed at the Wannsee Conference.

MARCH 1   Extermination by gas begins at Sobibor camp.

LATE MARCH   Deportations to Auschwitz begin.

JUNE 20   All Jewish schools closed.

JULY 28   Jewish fighting group organized in the Warsaw ghetto.

SUMMER   Dutch, Polish, French, Belgian, and Croatian Jews sent to extermination camps. Armed resistance by Jews in a few ghettos.

OCTOBER 4   All Jews in German concentration camps scheduled for transfer to Auschwitz.

NOVEMBER   Allied troops land in Africa.

WINTER   Norwegian, German, and Greek Jews sent to concentration camps. Jewish partisan groups gather in forests to fight.

1943

FEBRUARY 2   German army stopped at Stalingrad, Russia.

APRIL 19   Warsaw ghetto revolt begins. Jews fight until early June.

JUNE   Nazis order destruction of all ghettos in Poland and Russia. Armed resistance begins in many ghettos.

AUGUST 2   Armed revolt breaks out in Treblinka camp.

FALL   Large ghettos destroyed at Minsk, Vilna, and Riga. Danes begin the rescue of Danish Jewry.

OCTOBER 14   Armed revolt breaks out in Sobibor extermination camp.

1944

MARCH 19   Germany occupies Hungary.

MAY 15   Hungarian Jews are sent to concentration camps.

JUNE 6   Allies invade France.

JULY 24   Russian army liberates the concentration camp at Maidanek.

SUMMER   Remaining Jews in Kovno, Shavli, and Lodz ghettos are sent to concentration camps and the ghettos are destroyed.

OCTOBER 7   Revolt at Auschwitz.

OCTOBER 31   Remaining Slovakian Jews are sent to Auschwitz.

NOVEMBER 2   Jews remaining at Theresienstadt ghetto are sent to Auschwitz.

NOVEMBER 8   Beginning of death marches. 40,000 Jews are marched from Budapest to Austria.

1945

JANUARY 17   Auschwitz is abandoned by the Germans. Some prisoners begin death march toward Germany.

APRIL 6   Prisoners from Buchenwald begin four-day death march.

APRIL   Russian army enters Germany from the east as other Allied troops enter from the west.

APRIL 30   Hitler commits suicide in his underground bunker.

MAY 7   Germany surrenders. War in Europe ends.

AUGUST 15   Japan surrenders. World War II ends.

NOVEMBER 20   Nuremberg War Crimes Trials begin, ending on October 1, 1946.

SOURCES

Apion (quoted in Josephus, Against Apion, II, 8) cited in Edward H. Flannery, *The Anguish of the Jews: Twenty-Three Centuries of Anti-Semitism* (New York: The Macmillan Company, 1965).

Baker, Leonard, *Brandeis and Frankfurter: A Dual Biography* (New York: Harper & Row, 1984).

Bar Simeon, Salomon, as quoted in *International Anthology on Racism & Anti-Semitism*, edited by the International jCommittee of Educators to Combat Racism, Anti-Semitism and Apartheid (monograph: no date).

Berkowitz, Eliezer, *With God in Hell: Judaism in the Ghettos and Death-camps* (New York: Sanhedrin Press, 1979)

Bullock, Alan, "The Talents of Tyranny" in *The Nazi Revolution: Germany's Guilt or Germany's Fate?* edited by John L. Snell (Lexington, MA: D.C. Heath and Company, 1959)

Chartook, Roselle, and Jack Spencer, *The Holocaust Years: Society on Trial* (New York: Bantam Books, 1978).

Danziger Verposten, May 13, 1944.

Dawidowicz, Lucy S., *A Holocaust Reader* (New York: Behrman House, 1976).

Elenore, Lester, and Frederick E. Werbell, "The Lost Hero of the Holocaust—The Search for Sweden's Raoul Wallenberg," *The New York Times Magazine*, March 30, 1980.

Flender, Harold, *Rescue in Denmark*, (New York: Holocaust Library, 1963).

Forman, James D., *Nazism* (New York: Franklin Watts, 1978).

Frank, Anne, *The Diary of A Young Girl*, translated by B.M. Mooyaart-Doubleday (New York: Pocket Books, 1972).

Frideman, Phillip, *Their Brothers' Keepers* (New York: Holocaust Library, 1978).

Gilbert, Martin, *The Holocaust: A History of the Jews of Europe during the Second World War* (New York: Henry Holt and Company, 1985).

Gutman, Israel, editor, *Encyclopedia of the Holocaust*, Vol. 3 (New York: Macmillan Publishing Company, 1990).

Hausner, Gideon, *Justice in Jerusalem* (New York: Harper & Row, 1966).

Hilberg, Raul, *The Destruction of the European Jews* (New York: Franklin Watts, 1973).

Hitler, Adolf, *Mein Kampf*, translated by Ralph Manheim (New York: Houghton Mifflin, 1943).

International Military Tribunal: Nuremburg Official Text (English Edition, Vol. V., 10.

Laqueur, Walter, "Hitler's Holocaust: Who Knew What, When, & How?" in *Encounter* (Vol. LV, No. 1: July 1980).

Levi, Primo, *If This Is a Man* (New York: Orion Press, 1959).

Lookstein, Haskell, *Were We Our Brother's Keepers?* The Public Response of American Jews to the Holocaust, 1938-1944 (New York: Vintage Books, 1985).

Mlotek, Eleanor, and Malke Gottleib, editors, *We are Here: Songs of the Holocaust* (New York: Hippocrene Books, 1983).

Morse, Arthur D., *While Six Million died: A Cronicle of American Apathy* (New York: Hart Publishing Company, 1968).

Poliakov, Leon, *Harvest of Hate: The Nazi Program for the Destruction of the Jews of Europe* (New York: Holocaust Library, 1979).

Ringelblum, Emanuel, *Notes from the Warsaw Ghetto* (New York: McGraw Hill, 1958).

Robbin, Sheryl, "Life in the Camps: The Psychological Dimension" in Genocide: *Critical Issues of the Holocaust*, edited by Ales Grobman and Daniel Landes (Chappaqua, NY: Rossel Books, 1983).

Schoenberner, Gerhard, *The Yellow Star: The Perscution of the Jews in Europe, 1933-1945* (New York: Bantam Books, 1979).

Schlamm, Helmut, quoted in Byron L. Sherwin and Susan G. Ament, *Encountering the Holocaust: An Interdisciplinary Survey* (Chicago: Impact Press, 1979).

Smith, Bradley F., *Reaching Judgement at Nuremburg* (New York: New American Library, 1977).

Teaching about the Holocaust and Genocide: The Human Rights Series, Vol. 2, p. 43.

Thomas, Gordon and Max Morgan Witts, *Voyage of the Damned* (New York: Stein and Day, 1974).

The New Order by the Editors of Time-Life Books (Alexandria VA: Time-Life, 1988).

Trocme, Magda, quoted in Carol Rittner and Sondra Myers, *Courage to Care* (New York: New York University Press, 1986).

Webster's New Yorld Dictionary (New York: World Publishing Company, 1970).

Wermuth, Joshua, quoted in Yuri Suhl, *They Fought Back: The Story of the Jewish Resistance in Nazi Europe* (New York: Schocken Books, 1967).

SUGGESTIONS FOR FURTHER STUDY

New books about the Holocaust period are published continually. If you would like to study more about the Holocaust, you should consult your local Jewish or public library. The few books listed below are a good beginning.

Altshuler, David A. *Hitler's War Against the Jews.* New York: Behrman House, Inc., 1978

Berri, Claude. *The Two of Us.* New York: William Morrow, 1968.

Cowan, Lore. *Children of the Holocaust.* Des Moines, IA: Meredith, 1968.

Flinker, Moses. *Young Moshe's Diary.* New York: Doubleday, 1952.

Forman, James D. *Nazism.* New York: Franklin Watts, 1978.

Frank, Anne. *The Diary of a Young Girl.* New York: Pocket Books, 1952.

Friedman, Ina. *Escape or Die: True Stories of Young People Who Survived the Holocaust.* New York: Harper & Row, 1982.

Hoffman, Judith. *Joseph and Me.* Hoboken, NJ: KTAV Publishing, 1979.

I Never Saw Another Butterfly...: Children's Drawings and Poems from Terezin Concentration Camp, 1942-1944. New York: McGraw-Hill, 1971.

Lyttle, Richard B. *Nazi Hunting.* New York: Franklin Watts, 1982.

Meltzer, Milton. *Never to Forget: The Jews of the Holocaust.* New York: Harper & Row, 1976.

Reiss, Johanna. *The Upstairs Room.* New York: Thomas Y. Crowell, 1972.

Richter, Hans Peter. *Friedrich.* New York: Dell Publishing Company, 1970.

Romm, J. Leonard. *The Swastika on the Synagogue Door.* Chappaqua, NY: Rossel Books. 1984.

Rossel, Seymour. *The Holocaust: The Fire That Raged.* New York: Franklin Watts, 1969.

Shirer, William. *The Rise and Fall of Adolf Hitler.* New York: Random House, 1961.

Stadtler, Bea. *The Holocaust: A History of Courage and Resistance.* New York: Behrman House, Inc., 1961.

Suhl, Yuri. *On the Other Side of the Gate.* New York: Franklin Watts, 1973.

Tatelbaum, Itzak. *Through Our Eyes: Children Witness the Holocaust.* Jerusalem: I.B.T. Publishing, Inc., 1985.

Wiesel, Elie. *Night.* New York: Hill and Wang, 1960.

The following selections are for more advanced reading:

Fenelon, Fania and Routier, Marcelle. *Playing for Time.* New York: Atheneum, 1977.

Hersey, John. *The Wall.* New York: Alfred A. Knopf, 1950.

Klein, Gerda. *All But My Life.* New York: Hill and Wang, 1957.

Lustig, Arnost. *A Prayer for Katerina Horovitzova.* New York: Harper & Row, 1973.

Rubin, Ruth. *Voices of a People: The Story of Yiddish Folksong*, 2nd Ed. New York: McGraw-Hill, 1973.

Schwarz-Bart, Andre. *The Last of the Just.* New York: Atheneum, 1960.

Wiesel, Elie. *The Town Beyond the Wall.* New York: Holt, Rinehart and Winston, 1964.

Videocassettes of many major films are now locally available. The following films are based on Holocaust incidents. (Be certain to check film ratings for suitability.)

Animal Farm. C; 75 m. Directed by John Halas. British, 1955. Animated.

Cabaret. C; 128 m. Directed by Robert Fosse. US 1972. Winner of 8 Academy Awards.

The Diary of Anne Frank. B&W; 170 m. Directed by George Stevens. US, 1959. Winner of 3 Academy Awards.

The Garden of the Finzi-Continis. C; 95 m. Directed by Vittorio De Sica. Italian, 1971 Academy Award for Best Foreign Film.

Judgment at Nuremberg. B&W; 178 m. Directed by Stanley Kramer. US, 1961.

QB VII. C; 313 m. Directed by Tom Grief. US. 1974.

Ship of Fools. B&W; 149 m. Directed by Stanley Kramer. US, 1965. Winner of 2 Academy Awards.

The Two of Us. B&W; 86 m. Directed by Claude Berri. French, 1968.

Voyage of the Damned. C; 134 m. Directed by Stewart Rosenberg. British-Spanish, 1976.

INDEX